Pendulum and Divination

A Comprehensive Guide to Pendulums, and Other Future Prediction Methods

© Copyright 2023 - All rights reserved.

The content contained within this book may not be reproduced, duplicated, or transmitted without direct written permission from the author or the publisher.

Under no circumstances will any blame or legal responsibility be held against the publisher, or author, for any damages, reparation, or monetary loss due to the information contained within this book, either directly or indirectly.

Legal Notice:

This book is copyright protected. It is only for personal use. You cannot amend, distribute, sell, use, quote, or paraphrase any part, or the content within this book, without the consent of the author or publisher.

Disclaimer Notice:

Please note the information contained within this document is for educational and entertainment purposes only. All effort has been executed to present accurate, up-to-date, reliable, and complete information. No warranties of any kind are declared or implied. Readers acknowledge that the author is not engaging in the rendering of legal, financial, medical, or professional advice. The content within this book has been derived from various sources. Please consult a licensed professional before attempting any techniques outlined in this book.

By reading this document, the reader agrees that under no circumstances is the author responsible for any losses, direct or indirect, that are incurred as a result of the use of the information contained within this document, including, but not limited to, errors, omissions, or inaccuracies.

Free Bonus from Silvia Hill available for limited time

Hi Spirituality Lovers!

My name is Silvia Hill, and first off, I want to THANK YOU for reading my book.

Now you have a chance to join my exclusive spirituality email list so you can get the ebooks below for free as well as the potential to get more spirituality ebooks for free! Simply click the link below to join.

P.S. Remember that it's 100% free to join the list.

~~$27~~ **FREE BONUSES**

- 9 Types of Spirit Guides and How to Connect to Them
- How to Develop Your Intuition: 7 Secrets for Psychic Development and Tarot Reading
- Tarot Reading Secrets for Love, Career, and General Messages

Access your free bonuses here
https://livetolearn.lpages.co/pendulum-and-divination-paperback/

Table of Contents

PART 1: PENDULUM FOR BEGINNERS 1
   INTRODUCTION 2
   CHAPTER 1: A BRIEF HISTORY OF PENDULUMS 4
   CHAPTER 2: CHOOSING YOUR PENDULUM 13
   CHAPTER 3: PREPARATION AND CLEANSING 25
   CHAPTER 4: PROGRAMMING YOUR PENDULUM 32
   CHAPTER 5: PENDULUMS AND CRYSTALS 39
   CHAPTER 6: PENDULUMS FOR DOWSING AND DIVINATION 56
   CHAPTER 7: CREATE A PENDULUM CHART 66
   CHAPTER 8: PENDULUMS FOR SPIRITUAL HEALING 75
   CHAPTER 9: ENHANCING YOUR PENDULUM INTUITION 85
   CHAPTER 10: PENDULUM MAGIC 93
   CONCLUSION 104
PART 2: DIVINATION FOR BEGINNERS 106
   INTRODUCTION 107
   CHAPTER 1: DIVINATION NOW AND THEN 109
   CHAPTER 2: ASTROLOGY AND DIVINATION 119
   CHAPTER 3: DECODING YOUR BIRTH CHART 129
   CHAPTER 4: NUMEROLOGY 138
   CHAPTER 5: YOUR LIFE PATH NUMBER 146
   CHAPTER 6: THE DIVINING ART OF TAROT 154
   CHAPTER 7: HOW TO READ THE TAROT 163
   CHAPTER 8: PALMISTRY AND PALM READING 172

CHAPTER 9: RUNIC DIVINATION 182
CHAPTER 10: CRYSTAL DIVINATION 192
BONUS: GLOSSARY OF TERMS 200
CONCLUSION 206
HERE'S ANOTHER BOOK BY SILVIA HILL THAT YOU MIGHT
LIKE 208
FREE BONUS FROM SILVIA HILL AVAILABLE FOR LIMITED
TIME 209
REFERENCES 210

Part 1: Pendulum for Beginners

Unlocking the Secrets of Pendulums, Dowsing, Spiritual Healing, Magic, and Divination

Introduction

The pendulum has served as a tool for divination and dowsing rituals for thousands of years. Not only is it an incredible way to gain guidance in life, but it can also help locate resources, lost objects, and even people. Pendulums are considered one of the most utilized divinatory tools there is. Whether you're looking for simple yes/no answers to your questions, or a guided reading of your future, pendulums serve various purposes and are used in many rituals. Throughout history, pendulums have been used extensively and are now gaining attention again in the modern age. Their use is now accepted in numerous cultures and belief systems.

Although the pendulum is quickly gaining popularity, many people try using it briefly and then give up altogether. This is usually because they do not understand how to properly interpret pendulum readings and results. While using a pendulum seems simple in nature, you need patience, belief, knowledge, and, most of all, practice to get the best results. Once you're confident that a universal guide is working with you to give you answers, you'll start seeing viable results in no time.

This book is the perfect guide for your pendulum magic journey. Whether you want to learn about dowsing, healing magic, or divination rituals using pendulums, this book covers it all. Before we delve into pendulum rituals, it is important to understand where the concept of pendulums originated and when they began to be used for guidance purposes. To help you figure that out, the opening chapter of this book provides a detailed history of pendulums and their use through time so that you can begin your spiritual exploration journey on a solid basis.

Pendulums usually consist of a cone shape hung on a chain. Following that definition, anything can be a pendulum as long as one end of the chain is heavier and creates a swinging motion. There are various types of pendulums out there, each designed for special purposes, which will be discussed in detail in the upcoming chapters. Once you understand what type of pendulum you need for your ritual, you'll be ready to move on to the next part of the process. This will include cleansing and programming your pendulum to ensure no negative energies interfere and create an imbalance in your pendulum, thereby affecting the outcomes of your ritual.

In chapter 5, you'll be introduced to crystal pendulums and how to interpret their readings. After that, each chapter will define different pendulum magic rituals, including dowsing, divination, healing, balancing, intuition, and other magic rituals. There is also a chapter that provides detailed steps to make a pendulum chart for deeper readings and interpretations. Once you've gathered enough information about the specific process you plan to perform, all you need is a good pendulum that resonates with you and the intention to perform the ritual, which is the most important aspect of pendulum magic. If you're ready to explore this age-old instrument and discover how it can benefit you, by all means, keep reading!

Chapter 1: A Brief History of Pendulums

The opening chapter of this book is dedicated to pendulums and their use throughout history. Pendulums were traditionally used for a multitude of purposes, some of which are still applied today. Other practices related to this magical tool are fairly new. Dowsing is one of the most well-known applications of pendulums. However, there are plenty of other ways to incorporate this tool into your practice. To help you understand the concept behind their use, the following pages feature prime examples of how pendulums have helped people enhance this practice in both ancient and modern times.

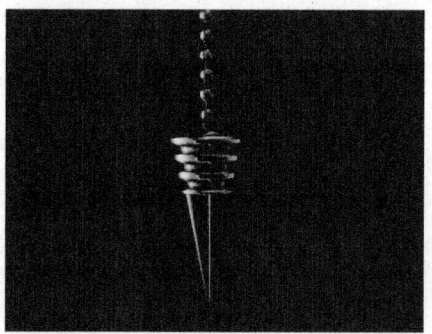

The key to choosing a pendulum is to find an object that lets the practitioner rely on their intuitive powers.
CC0 1.0 Universal (CC0 1.0) Public Domain Dedication
<https://creativecommons.org/publicdomain/zero/1.0/> https://www.pexels.com/photo/hanging-gold-colored-pendant-with-necklace-39239/

The Theory of Pendulum

A pendulum is a symmetrical, weighted tool attached to a single strand of cord or chain. Unlike similar magical objects, pendulums weren't made of metal or other magnetic materials. Instead, the item at the end of the cord was made from stone – usually a crystal with strong magical properties. These days, practitioners may also use metal balls, wooden beads, keys, and other trinkets of personal significance. Pendulums are used for spiritual guidance, to get answers to questions, to obtain help when making critical decisions, to cleanse your energy, and much more. Contemporary practitioners may also use it to find hidden objects, pets, and sources of illnesses or allergies in or near a person's body. Determining blockage, closing, or malfunction in your chakras (the body's primary energy centers) is another application of pendulum artistry used for healing purposes.

The key to choosing a pendulum is to find an object that lets the practitioner rely on their intuitive powers. The user can ask questions from their pendulum about the future or anything they may need guidance for. Holding the pendulum, they tap into their intuition. The object receives the information from the user's intuition, and by moving in a different direction, it lets the user know the answer to their question. It is believed that pendulums represent the physical manifestation of the user's soul, higher self, or, as it is called in modern times, their sixth sense. Pendulums can also help transmit information from spiritual guides, ancestors, and teachers.

Because it's a relatively simple tool, the question you ask your pendulum should also be simple. Beginners are generally advised to only ask questions that can be answered with a "yes" or "no." In contrast, advanced practitioners can also make more complex inquiries. Regardless of the complexity of the questions, they must be direct and backed up by strong intent. Pendulums connect the rational (conscious) side of the brain with the intuitive (subconscious) one, provided there is a powerful intent to do so on the rational side. When these two elements are connected, you can tap into your intuition and confidently make every decision – unlike when you rely only on the rational part of your mind.

That said, the artistry of pendulum use requires a little practice and plenty of trust in your gut instincts. People often believe that the tool only responds to the small movements of nerves in the practitioner's hand and nothing more. It may take opening one's mind to accept where the answers come from, especially if you also want to access information from other higher beings and not just your intuition.

What Is Dowsing?

Dowsing is an ancient divination form that uses tools like bobbers, Y rods, L rods, and pendulums. It's one of the simplest forms of divination using pendulums. The tools were traditionally made by the practitioner, although nowadays, you can buy them online or from any well-equipped shop selling magical supplies. In case you want to make your own tools, you'll also find plenty of information about it to help you out. That way, you'll feel more connected to your pendulum, which goes a long way in learning to rely on your intuition.

As with learning to use any other magical tool, mastering dowsing with pendulums requires grounding, focus, intention, intuitive listening skills, and practice. Practitioners typically learn dowsing by asking the pendulum simple and trivial questions. You definitely want to know more about tapping into your intuition before you place your future on the line. Typically, the user would seek an answer before deciding between two choices, so the pendulum would only confirm the answer from these two options. Depending on which way the pendulum swings, you can find answers to questions such as buying or selling something, spending money one way or another, moving or staying to live in one place, changing your job or not, etc.

How practitioners decipher their messages depends on how determined they are to see the pendulum's movements. For example, practitioners may interpret swinging in a clockwise direction as a "yes," and a simple left-to-right movement as a "no." Others may choose to see these responses the other way around. Even knowing that, at the beginning of your learning journey, you may get unclear answers, which is entirely normal – it simply means you'll have to practice some more. Practitioners also recommend honing one's grounding skills to obtain accurate information.

That said, no matter how you practice it, dowsing won't give you information as precise as the name of the person you'll meet any time from now or even the date you'll meet them. However, if you're making a decision about who to ask for help and you have two names in mind, the pendulum can help you pick the right person. Dowsing has also been used for developing one's intuition. It can help open the chakras, allowing the user to direct their energy through their body, manipulate it, and enhance it during magical practices or throughout life in general.

The History of Pendulum Practice

The practice of dowsing can be traced back to ancient times and is even recorded in the Bible. The earliest known pendulums were made from flexible papyrus fronds. The material allowed them to spin and sway at the same time. In the Bible, this motion has been described as rods being turned into serpents, showing the requested information with their slithering movements. One of the historical figures to have used this technique was Moses, who applied it to find water in the desert.

Historical evidence of dowsing with pendulums was documented in 400 BCE when the Pythian Oracle of Delphi applied this art to seek answers about the future. King Alfred the Great (848-899 AD) was fascinated by the practice of dowsing, and he immortalized it in the piece he commissioned to be made. The figure holds two objects (known as the Alfred Jewel) crossed and pointing in a direction that indicates answers. There are also records of pendulums being used in Ancient Rome and Egypt. A couple of centuries later, in the late 1500s, Italian scientist Galileo Galilei studied the art of pendulum use and made a report that many other European scientists took advantage of. One of these scientists was a polymath, Leonardo Davinci. Around the same time, Queen Elizabeth I became interested in dowsing, inviting several French and German dowsers to instruct her. This reportedly led to the development of copper and tin mining practices in Cornwall.

By the mid-1600s, dowsing was widely used to find lucrative mining places for precious metals, including gold. However, the practice also reached a point where the Catholic Church found it necessary to ban it. Although criticism directed toward pendulums and dowsing was nothing new (Pope John XXII had already declared its users to be witches in the 1300s), in the 17th century, it was associated with the occult and was labeled a diabolical practice along with several other witchcraft practices. While the allegations of the Church are still considered unfounded, it was enough to subdue pendulum dowsing for a while.

In 1833, French chemist Michel-Eugène Chevreul researched the pendulum's movement. He found that the tool actually moved due to the involuntary reflexes of the user's hand. This movement is known today as the "ideomotor reflex," triggered by subconscious thoughts and emotions, also known as intuition. Chevreul also established that the pendulum responds to the changes in a person's energetic field, representing the spiritual manifestation of their higher self and intuition. Once a piece of information leaves the hidden depths of the subconscious mind, this triggers a reflex in the practitioner's arm, moving the pendulum in their hand. This confirmed the theory that while the muscles and nerves move the arm, they could only do so due to the intuitive activity of the person's brain. After this discovery, the use of pendulums again started to gain popularity, and scientists took a renewed interest in studying how this magical tool harnesses information from one's intuition.

Abbe Mermet, a French priest, also took an interest in pendulums in the early 20th century. Inspired by the story of Moses, Mermet pioneered a pendulum to find water and minerals in the African deserts. He dowsed by swinging the pendulum over a map, relying on his intuition to find the object of his inquiries. Later, he was asked to find missing persons and was even commissioned by the Vatican to solve archaeological issues for the city-state. Mermet also dowsed for the location of illnesses or injuries in the human body, making him one of the pioneers of modern exploratory diagnostics. Although this practice is believed to have been used since ancient times, Mermet was honored for his work.

Dowsing was also used in World War II by Abbe Bouly, who served as an explorer for mines on the beaches of France. His efforts led to saving thousands of soldiers' lives, for which he was honored by Pope Pius XII. Around the same time, Alfred Bovis, a French food taster, developed the Bovis Biometer. This device measures the energy that radiates from objects. This device used to rate the vibrational energy of food was a pendulum made of quartz crystal, still used by modern food scientists.

In the 1950s, Evelyn Penrose used pendulum dowsing to communicate with animals to heal them and learn more about them. Known today as "animal whisperers," this is another practice that has gained popularity in modern times. Penrose also used pendulums to help resolve water source issues that several governments faced during that time. In fact, she would often dowse over the map of a country in her home, and once she located water, she would visit the location she had found.

Ernest Hartmann was a notable pendulum dowser throughout the 20th century who was also involved in finding water. He became known for mapping out underground water lines and pointing out areas where no water could be found. He established that these areas were out of balance energy-wise and could potentially disrupt the entire environment surrounding them. Furthermore, 21st-century scientists have discovered that living in these areas harms people's health. This phenomenon was coined "geopathic stress."

Pendulums and dowsing can be used for many purposes, and modern applications are constantly being developed. Modern devices are often built to follow the same energetic principles as applied in dowsing. In the upcoming section, you'll see some of the ways pendulums can be used for contemporary purposes. However, the list of applications is still growing and is expected to keep growing.

Modern Uses for Pendulums

Pendulums remain powerful magical tools any contemporary practitioner can use for numerous purposes. Here are some ways pendulums are used in modern times.

Finding Lost Objects

To employ the pendulum to find lost belongings, pets, people, or a place to stay, practitioners often use it over maps. They lay the map out on a table and move the pendulum over it while asking the tool to show the direction in which what they need lies. They'll find the object in that direction depending on whether it swings east, north, south, or west. Next, the practitioners will narrow down the space on the map and ask the pendulum whether the object in question is found in a specific place. They can even follow up with more specific questions, like confirming the name of the street or shop where the object may be located.

Self-Improvement

Modern practitioners often use pendulums for guidance when making life-changing decisions. For example, a person seeking professional advancement may consult a pendulum about potential new jobs they can apply for. They can see which position would be the most fulfilling for them while helping them hone their skills or develop new ones. Pendulums typically confirm answers you are already contemplating – even if only subconsciously. At other times, the answers one gets from the pendulum can be rather surprising. Fresh college graduates who contemplate continuing their studies often check with their pendulum to see whether it's the right decision. Several cases have been recorded when the pendulum advised against this decision and pointed to either getting a job, traveling, or pursuing other adventures. In these cases, the graduates only wanted to continue their studies because they didn't consciously know what else to do and not because they found studying a rewarding way to spend their time. Bearing this in mind, their pendulum helped them find a more fulfilling path.

Improving Physical and Mental Health

Those struggling to get fit, lose weight, or simply improve their physical health can consult a pendulum to resolve their issues. For example, suppose a person is unsure which activity will help them achieve their goals. In that case, they can ask the pendulum about the benefits of different exercises. Pendulums can also help find ideal relaxation methods and ways to establish a healthy sleep pattern, diet, and lifestyle in general. It can also answer questions about improving cognitive functions, which is another great way to keep your mental health in check. Experienced practitioners know how to tune their bodies to the pendulum's movement, allowing them to use their bodies instead of a pendulum. They simply close their eyes and let their body sway towards or away from the object, symbol, or activity in question.

Emotional and Spiritual Growth

If a practitioner has trouble finding the appropriate way to express their emotions, the pendulum can show it to them. For example, if someone is used to expressing their strong feelings about a particular topic but isn't sure if they should, consulting a pendulum can advise them against forcefully voicing their opinion – but also encourage them to find other ways to articulate what's on their mind. Sometimes, the pendulum will tell a person to speak up rather than bottle up their emotions. This leads to a balanced emotional life and the acquisition of emotional control skills. Pendulums can also help locate new spiritual beliefs and ideologies you can identify with. Spirituality, as the expression of your soul's desires, is fertile ground for dowsing and other pendulum divination practices. When you find the belief that aligns with your values, a pendulum can give a clear answer regarding whether the belief in question is suitable.

Affirmation Practices

Pendulums are widely known for their use in modern affirmation practices. And it doesn't take much to get revealing answers. Typically, the practitioner will simply sit and repeat an affirmation similar to this one:

"I have a good life because I have everything I need – success, happiness, and prosperity in all areas that matter."

Even if the person hasn't got everything going on great for them at present, affirming it can help them manifest the desired state in the future. This is because the more they repeat the affirmative statement, the more it stays ingrained in their subconscious. Over time, the conscious mind takes over, encouraging the person to seek action that enables the success, happiness, and prosperity they've manifested. It often only takes finding what you truly love doing in life to achieve all three of the desired states. As it happens, pendulums can show you how to find the purpose that leads to this.

Creating Spaces

Creating or finding the most appropriate space for living or your business is another great example of pendulum artistry. From putting together timeless decor to allowing the energy to flow freely through your home, pendulums can show you everything you need to know about arranging your space. The same applies to plants and herbs in your garden. If you want to know which plants you should add to your garden to enrich your practices, you must ask the pendulum. Not only that, but it's also believed that pendulums can help you communicate with plants. This idea is rooted in the experiment performed by Cleve Backster in 1966. Backster was an expert in the field of lie detectors who accidentally discovered that plants can provide an emotional response when threatened with abuse. They can pick up human emotions and react to them accordingly. This is what pendulums enhance as well.

Influencing the Conscious through Magic

While the answers come from the subconscious, a person can direct their conscious mind to influence their subconscious in a direction that makes their desires come true. In other words, by impacting the conscious, you can also promote the manifestation of the desires hidden in your subconscious. Contemporary practitioners often use pendulums to uncover their desires and place them in their conscious minds. Some of the most common desires for people are:

- Loving, affectionate, and accepting relationships
- A vacation that allows for ultimate relaxation
- A safe and comfortable living space
- Lasting physical, mental and emotional health
- Financial, academic, and professional prosperity

Practitioners often find that what they are looking for typically falls into these categories, even if they weren't aware of this. It's not uncommon for people to realize that what they thought they needed isn't what they truly desire. At other times, the pendulum will help manifest exactly what people want. The best example would be Conrad Hilton, who carried a photograph of a prestigious hotel in his pocket. From time to time, he took out the picture and dowsed a pendulum to reinforce his desire to establish his own hotel. One day, his dream came true, and he became the owner of a global luxury hotel chain.

Chapter 2: Choosing Your Pendulum

Choosing your pendulum is the most important step of the process. The type of pendulum you select will depend on various factors. Many people are confused when choosing a pendulum for their spiritual and healing practices, which is understandable considering the extensive styles of pendulums available. Picking the right pendulum is crucial to the success of the process, whether you want to practice dowsing, grounding, or healing pendulum magic. So, while choosing your pendulum is a vital process, nothing stops it from being a fun experience.

Choosing your pendulum is the most important step of the process.
https://www.pexels.com/photo/woman-telling-fortune-with-silver-pendant-7391635/

While many people are curious about pendulum selection, there are no hard and fast rules that must be followed in this case. The choice depends on different factors, which will be discussed in this chapter. The final decision will ultimately come down to your preference.

When selecting your pendulum, it is essential to ensure that you're attracted to the pendulum and find it absorbing. This experience will differ for everyone, which is why there are no immutable rules surrounding this process. However, understanding the different types of pendulums and when they are most useful will come in handy when picking your pendulum. This chapter will introduce the numerous styles of pendulums available and explain what factors you should consider before selecting one. A pendulum selection checklist is also included at the end of the chapter.

If you're a beginner, one of the best pendulum styles uses a triangular or teardrop shape of a suitable material. What's great about these pendulums is that they don't weigh a lot and can easily be rotated. Plus, they won't cost you a fortune. That said, remember that this type of pendulum may not be suitable for you or compatible with the process you're going to practice. Bearing this in mind, it's critical that the pendulum you choose feels right for you and suits the purposes you have in mind.

Factors to Consider for Choosing a Pendulum

While there are countless factors you can consider when selecting a pendulum, the primary considerations should include the weight, shape, and material of the pendulum. These elements must be taken into account because they play a vital role in how the healing or other pendulum magic processes take place and their effectiveness.

1. **Weight**

Considering the pendulum's weight is of utmost importance when selecting one for any spiritual process. If you choose a heavy pendulum, you'll have to put in more effort during your practice. On the upside, heavy pendulums have the benefit of stronger feedback from these practices. The only downside is that you'll have to pay more attention to the pendulum. Otherwise, you risk losing control of it during practice.

By contrast, a lighter pendulum would be much easier to handle but will not provide the same level of connection as a heavier one. For example, suppose you're practicing dowsing with a light pendulum. In that case, you will not feel the same level of connection as you would with a heavy pendulum.

You can also try a medium-weighted pendulum, whose speed is neither too fast nor too slow, which gives the perfect response time compared to other pendulums. Their movement along the axis will also be just the right speed for a meaningful response.

2. Shape

Pendulums come in a plethora of shapes ranging from circular to angular ones. Others can be combination shapes merged together. Round pendulums are said to have a more feminine energy, whereas rectangular or square-shaped pendulums manifest more masculine energy. For example, a round dome ceiling seems more feminine when compared to the square top of a skyscraper. However, each of these shapes has a different vibe and cannot be completely classified as masculine or feminine.

The shape of a pendulum is a major consideration because the manifestation of energy produced by the pendulum depends on its structure. When selecting a shape, there's not much to remember except what feels genuinely attractive to your soul. Moreover, the pendulum's movement will also depend on what shape you select.

If you're selecting a pendulum specifically for the purpose of dowsing, opt for one that will move in imperfect circles during the process. To that end, try positioning the pendulum you're selecting the same way you would hold it while dowsing; then observe its path of motion. The pendulum doesn't necessarily have to be circular for this purpose, but it shouldn't be a shape that doesn't have a smooth, consistent rotation.

You'll witness that some of the commercially designed pendulums have a hollow compartment inside. These are called sample pendulums and are usually used to locate things. The hollow space is provided for you to put a sample of whatever it is you're searching for inside. For instance, if you're searching for water, put a small amount inside the pendulum's hollow portion. Similarly, insert oil if you're trying to locate oil using pendulum magic. Most basic shapes include drop-shaped, mermet-shaped, rectangular-shaped with hollow compartments, and crystal pendulums.

3. Material

A whole range of materials can be used to design the perfect pendulums for healing and spiritual practices. Usually, these pendulums are made of wood, brass, crystals, or other metals. Now, do you know which material works best for you? Since each type has specially defined purposes, when selecting your pendulum, keep a list of your requirements with you to find the most suitable one for your practice.

4. Brass

Brass pendulums are a superb choice when you need something durable. Although they will weigh more against other types of pendulums, their metallic nature inhibits any external energies from being absorbed into their structure. Therefore, these pendulums have neutral energy and don't need regular cleansing. Moreover, their movements are also suitable for different divination processes.

5. Stainless Steel

There are countless steel and stainless steel pendulums of various shapes. The best part about these pendulums is that they're made with different metals, including iron, nickel, chromium, silicon, and aluminum, which makes them more energy-conducive than their regular metal counterparts. Plus, many spiral-caged pendulums are designed to have a crystal placed within them. With that, you'll have the conductivity of both the metal and the crystal you decide to place. The best part is that it's very versatile. This way, you won't have to collect numerous crystal pendulums and can settle for a single steel pendulum and collect different crystals separately.

6. Wood

Wooden pendulums are usually designed to be bigger in size than their brass or crystal counterparts, but they're relatively lighter in weight. Like brass pendulums, wooden pendulums also have neutral energies and don't need to be cleansed as often as other materials. Wood is a durable material that will last longer if not exposed to water or other liquids. Plus, their response timing and position are superior to most pendulum materials.

7. Crystal

Many practitioners often prefer crystal pendulums due to their appealing structures and excellent response time. However, crystal pendulums tend to be more fragile in nature compared to brass or wood pendulum. So, if you drop it or slam it against something, cracks will likely form on the surface.

The best part about crystal pendulums is that they each manifest a different kind of energy. Crystal pendulums will have a distinctively unique energy signature, unlike other pendulum materials. For example, rose quartz is linked to the heart chakra and should be the crystal material of choice for relationship-related divination practices.

The specific attributes associated with the kind of crystal pendulum you select will determine the outcome of your practice. Many people even prefer to use their crystal pendulums as necklaces or charms and wear them as personal items. This is why selecting the one that matches your personality and doesn't hamper your natural energy is essential.

Unlike brass and wooden pendulums, crystal pendulums need to be cleansed to get rid of accumulated external energies. Crystal pendulums are so versatile that a whole chapter is dedicated to that topic later in the book. For a summary of the crystal types, you can consult the following table:

	Crystal	Association
1.	Agate	Balance, victory, protection
2.	Agate, Eye	Spiritual connection
3.	Agate, Moss	Relocation, new beginnings, job, house
4.	Amazonite	Creativity, communication, confidence
5.	Amber	Past
6.	Amethyst	Spiritual connection, psychic abilities, healing
7.	Aquamarine	Protection, peace, balanced emotions, elimination of fear

	Crystal	Association
8.	Aventurine	Good fortune, good health, centering
9.	Beryl	Psychic awareness, creative opening, discovery
10.	Bloodstone	Prosperity, good health, protection from deceit and deception
11.	Carnelian	Protection from evil, confidence, and balancing
12.	Chalcedony	Aura cleansing, protection during travels
13.	Chrysocolla	Communication, protection, tension release
14.	Chrysoprase	Truth revelations, balancing
15.	Citrine	Prosperity, self-esteem, karmic lessons
16.	Fluorite	Grounding, healing, cleansing, past lives
17.	Hematite	Stress relief, grounding, courage
18.	Jade, blue	Relaxation, karmic influences
19.	Jade, green	Protection from evil, relaxation
20.	Jade, brown	Grounding, stabilizing
21.	Jasper, red	Protection from negative energies

	Crystal	Association
22.	Jasper, green	Healing, balancing
23.	Jasper, brown	Grounding, stabilizing
24.	Labradorite	Spiritual connection
25.	Lapis lazuli	Psychic abilities, creativity, anxiety relief
26.	Malachite	Healing, evil repellent
27.	Obsidian, black	Eliminates negativity
28.	Obsidian, snowflake	Prosperity, protection, balancing
29.	Onyx, black	Destruction of negative energies
30.	Quartz, clear	Protection, spiritual connection
31.	Quartz, rose	Love, healing, balance
32.	Quartz, smoky	Grounding, centering, strengthening
33.	Tiger's eye	Insight, good luck, previous lives
34.	Tourmaline	Calming, clarity, success, good fortune, balance
35.	Turquoise	Balance, communication, protection, psychic connection

Selection of Pendulum Based on Its Use

Considering the primary goal of your pendulum, magic is essential before you can go about choosing one for the process. The material of the pendulum gives it unique properties that affect the final outcome of the divination or healing practice. This section will help you identify the optimal type of pendulum for your intended practice.

1. Healing

If the purpose of your pendulum magic is healing, balancing, or clearing spiritual blockages, you'll need to choose crystals that are linked to the chakras in question. Different crystals are associated with the seven chakras and are used to help them align, clear, or balance. You can also opt for copper or brass pendulums when planning to do an energy healing practice. The following table shows the seven chakras and the crystals associated with each of them:

	Chakras	Associated crystals
1.	Crown chakra	Clear quartz, moonstone, labradorite, amethyst
2.	Third eye chakra	Lapis lazuli, azurite
3.	Throat chakra	Turquoise, blue agate, aquamarine
4.	Heart chakra	Rose quartz, green agate, amazonite
5.	Solar plexus chakra	Citrine, amber, tiger's eye
6.	Sacral chakra	Carnelian, tiger's eye
7.	Root chakra	Black obsidian, tourmaline, bloodstone

2. Divination

If divination is your intended purpose, select a pendulum that can conduct higher spiritual energies and enhance your psychic abilities. It should also protect the wearer from any negative energies. You can refer to the list above to select a crystal suitable for this purpose. Usually, clear quartz pendulums are used for divination purposes. Not only can it conduct energy and transform it, but it also intensifies the energy, enhancing your abilities.

Another commonly used tool in divination includes the Merkaba pendulum. This type of pendulum helps connect with spiritual guides and establish universal connections. It is considered a multidimensional vessel that allows a link to be formed between different dimensions while also protecting the user. This type of pendulum also enables the brain to become more creative and solve problems.

Other crystals include Sheesham or Indian rosewood, which is connected to femininity. Associated with the heart chakra, this crystal pendulum is used to meditate when struggling with hindrances.

Using More Than One Pendulum

If you plan to practice dowsing, you can use multiple pendulums for this purpose. Instead of ordering a different pendulum for a certain purpose every time, get multiple pendulums and add them to your collection. You'll find that certain pendulums are more suited than others for specific tasks. This is why it's necessary to have a variety of crystals and other pendulums on hand. You can also use more than one pendulum together – try different combinations of crystals and see which ones work out best for you.

For beginners, a basic pendulum collection will typically include a teardrop-shaped pendulum, a triangular crystal pendulum, a conical beechwood pendulum, and a brass pendulum. That said, you're not strictly limited to these pendulums and can choose from the plethora of types available. Asking fellow enthusiasts or searching for recommendations online can help expand your horizons and allow you to make suitable acquisitions.

Bonus: Make Your Own Pendulum

While choosing a pendulum for divination and healing is a fun experience in itself, what's better than making your own pendulum from scratch? This can seem out of reach for beginners, but it really isn't. Crafting a pendulum at home is not as complicated as it sounds and takes just a few steps. Plus, this way, you'll have a deeper and more meaningful connection with your pendulum compared to a ready-bought one. You'll feel a sense of ownership of the pendulum and likely get a better response. You can make crystal and wooden pendulums with just a few basic supplies. Here's how to do it:

Crystal Pendulum

To craft a crystal pendulum, you'll need the following:

- Your preferred crystal or gemstone
- A thin wire or string
- A lightweight chain (metallic)
- Glue (optional)
- Sharp scissors

To make the pendulum:

1. Grab the wire and wrap it around the crystal until it forms a stronghold. Leave enough wire length at the end to form a loop. Alternatively, you can use glue to attach the crystal to the wire. Make sure you cut off any ends of the wire that are sticking out.

2. Bend the wire at the end to form a small loop. Connect one end of the chain on this loop and let the other end stay as it is. Make sure the length of the chain doesn't exceed 30cm or 12in.

3. To calibrate the pendulum, rest your elbow on a table, and hold the chain slightly above the table's surface. Decide which swing motions would be "yes," "no," or "unknown." For example, left to right motion can be yes, while up and down motion can mean no, and a circular motion could mean unknown.

4. Keep the pendulum perfectly still, and ask a basic question you know the answer to. For example, you can ask, "Is the sky blue?" which you know is true.

5. Observe the pendulum's motion and see if it swings in the right direction. If not, try with another question or another material until

you get an appropriate response.

Wooden Pendulum

To craft a wooden pendulum, you'll need the following:

- Thin, dry twigs
- Fine saw
- One small eye screw
- Woodburning tools
- Woodworking drill
- Sandpaper
- Waxed cotton cord

To make the pendulum:

1. You can use different kinds of wood to make this pendulum. Some people believe that different types of wood are used for certain purposes. So, use whatever type you deem appropriate. Make sure the twigs are dry and as straight as possible; this will help shape the pendulum. Try not to use freshly cut twigs, as they can break easily.

2. Firstly, remove the bark from the twigs using sandpaper. Make sure you use rougher sandpaper before moving on to finer ones. Keep scraping until the bark comes off completely and you get a smooth wooden surface. Also, straighten the twig when you're scraping off the bark.

3. Next, using sandpaper, you need to sharpen all four sides of the twig from one end. However, stop and check each side to ensure they're all even.

4. After you've created a tip, it's time to round it out by rubbing the twig on the sandpaper. Make a rolling movement with the twig over the sandpaper. However, make sure the tip becomes perfectly round while also staying even. This step could take a while, but the end result will be worth it.

5. Once you're satisfied with how the tip of the pendulum looks, cut the desired length of the wood for your pendulum. You can use a fine saw for this purpose.

6. Now, work the sandpaper over the other end of the pendulum to get a round end on the other side. Make sure you get a smooth

finish before moving on to decorating.

7. It's not necessary to decorate the pendulum. Still, it will certainly make it look better and bring you closer to your homemade magical tool. Using a woodburning tool, you can draw various patterns, symbols, and signs on the wooden pendulum.
8. Before drawing the permanent patterns on the pendulum, sketch out rough patterns using a pencil. Once you're satisfied with your drawings, it's time to make the final patterns using the woodburning tool. Make sure you don't apply too much pressure during this step.
9. Add in details, correct any mistakes, and take a final look at your work. You can also paint the wood using poster paints or use spray paint.
10. Now, drill a hole at the top of the pendulum (the rounded part) and attach the eye bolt. Make sure it is secure before inserting the chain or string through it. Use liquid glue if necessary.
11. Now, put the string through the loop, and add other small trinkets and decorations if desired.

Choosing a pendulum is the first step in pendulum magic, healing, and divination. As daunting as it can be for a beginner to select their first pendulum, it can be a fun and enriching experience. Selecting your pendulum requires great thought, care, and consideration. As you've seen, certain factors shouldn't be neglected when choosing your pendulums. Otherwise, the results of your readings could be disturbed. So, make sure your account for the pendulum's intended purpose before considering other important factors like weight, shape, and material. Understanding the various crystal types and how they can help with different spiritual and divination purposes is also important. In the end, don't overthink the process. If a pendulum calls out to you, you should definitely consider it for your practice, no matter the odds.

Chapter 3: Preparation and Cleansing

As you know by now, pendulums manifest energy not just on their own but also from their surrounding environment. This can be neutral, negative, or positive energy absorbed from various people and places before the pendulum gets to you. For instance, imagine that your pendulum was handmade with love by someone. It is likely to possess an abundance of positive energy. By contrast, if it was prepared or even simply packaged by someone going through difficult circumstances, the pendulum likely absorbed negative emotions and despairing energy.

A pendulum's energy should be cleansed and cleared like you cleanse your own aura.
https://www.pexels.com/photo/woman-meditating-with-pendulum-8770828/

This is why cleaning the pendulum before performing any divination is essential, even if you're using it for the first time. You never know where the pendulum had been before arriving at your doorstep. If you begin using it before any cleansing process, you'll likely get inaccurate and strange results or no results. A pendulum's energy should be cleansed and cleared in the same way you cleanse your own aura.

When you feel low, grumpy, or extremely pessimistic, it's clear that some negative forces are affecting your energy field. The same goes for divinatory tools, which need to be cleansed to eliminate any external energies to work perfectly. Fortunately, there are many ways you can do that. This chapter will go into detail about different cleansing techniques you can apply not just for your pendulums but for any other divinatory tools.

However, the single most important element of these techniques is your intention. The first step before any cleansing process is to set the intention for the practice. How do you do that? It's quite simple. First, you'll need to gather the materials you'll be using in the process. These could include salt, smudge sticks, water, soil, crystals, etc. Once you've done that, place the cleansing tool with your pendulum, close your eyes, and set the intention to remove unwanted energies from your pendulum with the help of the tools you're using.

Make sure you set the intention with kind words and thoughts instead of exhibiting stern behavior. If you set intentions in a bad mood, often, the purpose gets completed but not in an optimal way. So, it's better to avoid bad intentions. At last, you can start cleansing your pendulum in any of the ways described below:

1. Smoke

Smoke from smudge sticks has long been used to cleanse and clear energy. This tradition goes back to the Native Americans who used it to cleanse their auras. Usually, smudge sticks are made using sage, specifically white sage, but you can also use other herbs. These include rosemary, palo santo, lavender, eucalyptus, mugwort, sweetgrass, cedar, and any other herbs that boast cleansing properties.

How does smoke cleansing using herbs work? Basically, the negative ions of the smoke attach themselves to the positive ions floating around the aura of the tool that needs cleansing, which in this case, is a pendulum. Once these ions are removed, their energy is neutralized and stops affecting the performance of the pendulum. Because of this, the negative ions of the smoke take away the positive ions from the affected material and store this energy in the earth for transmutation.

To perform the cleansing process with smudge sticks, you must take the necessary safety precautions to ensure you don't end up hurting yourself or setting your house on fire. To do this, keep a heatproof bowl below the smudge stick while practicing the cleansing technique. This will ensure you catch any embers that fly out of the smudge stick. Once you light the smudge stick, don't blow it out instantly – let the flame die out by itself or shake it out. After this, you'll see a waft of smoke emanating from the stick. This is when you place the pendulum above the stick so that the smoke engulfs the pendulum. You'll know that the cleansing process has been successful by observing the color and movement of the smoke. If the smoke is thick and dark, there's a lot of energy left to clear, and when it becomes lighter, the energy has been cleared.

The movement of the smoke will also change once the pendulum has been cleansed. The smoke should move away from the pendulum once all negative energies have been evacuated. If you're in a room, make sure you open all the windows to let the smoke and negative energies leave the room. Once the process is done, leave the smudge stick in the heatproof bowl to burn out, or extinguish it with some sand.

2. Sunlight or Moonlight

One of the best and most effective ways to cleanse your pendulum of negative energy is through moonlight or sunlight. To cleanse under the moonlight, you'll have to do so on a full moon. This is because the full moon is the optimal time to release anything negative in your life. It is said that the moon is at its fullest power during the full moon and can pull all sorts of negative energies from the earth, just like it pulls the tides. So, if you want to cleanse your pendulum of negative energy, a full moon ritual is the perfect way to achieve that. To do this, you'll first need to set the intention of the ritual and then bring out your pendulum. Next, dip the pendulum into the purest water you can find, and make sure you do this under the moonlight. Once you're sure it's clean, remove it and dry it completely to prevent the metallic chain from rusting. Place the pendulum right under the moonlight, whether it's outside your house, on the roof, or simply on your windowsill. Retrieve the pendulum the next morning after dawn.

Alternatively, you can use sunlight as a technique to cleanse your pendulum of any negative energy. Sunlight is said to rejuvenate, recharge, and refresh objects. To perform this process, you must leave your pendulum in direct sunlight for a few hours. However, be mindful that this process is a bit harsher than moonlight rituals and should only last 3 to 4 hours. Some crystals like amethyst, rose quartz, citrine, and smoky quartz can fade if kept out in the sun for too long. Another thing you should be careful of is that some crystals in the quartz family can cause a fire when focusing on direct sunlight, so be mindful about where and how you place them.

3. Soil

Soil is one of the natural resources we can use to cleanse the negative energies of our divination tools. It not only helps grow, nourish, and ground energy but also clears any negative frequencies as well. To perform a soil cleansing, set the intention of clearing out negative energies from the pendulum and releasing them into the earth for transmutation. This process is said to be especially powerful for natural materials like crystal pendulums.

To perform the cleansing, place the pendulum in the soil of a potted plant or simply in open soil in your garden or yard. Leave it there for a few days until you feel that the negative energy has cleared away. Some people prefer to leave their pendulums in the dirt for a whole moon cycle to ensure all the negative entities have left the pendulum. When that is done, remove the pendulum from the dirt, and thank the earth for its favor.

4. Salt

Salt is considered an effective purifier and has been used to cleanse and clear away negative energies for centuries. Many people use it to ward off negative energy. Salt acts as a barrier to any negative or nasty energies, making it an ideal medium to cleanse your pendulum of inauspicious energy. You'll need a small bowl filled with sea salt or Himalayan salt to do this. Place the pendulum on top of the salt, or bury it underneath the mound of salt. Leave this overnight. Retrieve the pendulum the next morning with a cleansed, refreshed energy. Alternatively, you can mix salt with water and pour it over the pendulum to cleanse it. Another method of salt cleansing involves collecting seawater in a jar and using it to cleanse your pendulum's energy. However, if the chain of your pendulum is silver, salt cleansing is not a suitable method, as it can cause the chain to rust.

5. Water

Using water to purify and cleanse your pendulums is a great way to sift out all the negative energies that manifest themselves in them. Cleaning your pendulums with water isn't just good for when you need to cleanse them but also when other people have touched them. Since you don't want anyone else's energy on your pendulum, it's best to clean it right then and there. For the cleansing process, find the purest water you can find and run it over the pendulum. Suppose you have access to natural flowing springs or streams. In that case, that's even better because the water comes from Mother Nature herself. If not, use filtered or purified water for the best results.

In parallel, visualize white light while cleansing your pendulum with water, and imagine it flowing through the water over it. Unlike other cleansing techniques, you don't need to submerge the pendulum under water for long periods. Simply running water over the pendulum will suffice to restore balance to the pendulum's energies.

6. Light and Visualization

Visualization is an essential yet often underappreciated activity. In today's world, we only ever use the logical and analytical parts of the brain, often forgetting about the creative part. Using a visualization method to cleanse your pendulums will be fun and bring out your creative side. If you're not used to visualization, it's better to practice it first for a few days before you try this cleansing ritual on your pendulum.

You can do this by sitting outside in a calm atmosphere, closing your eyes, and imagining a white light descending from the sky and settling around you. Once you start feeling an energy shift, your process will be successful. The more you perform this exercise, the more easily the visualized light will come to you. You can also try to visualize other colors as well. Still, the most suitable color is white, as it symbolizes purity, peace, protection, and serenity. Other colors signify:

- **Yellow:** Intellect, strength, energy
- **Green:** Luck, fortune, prosperity, abundance, balance, healing
- **Orange:** Luck, confidence, success
- **Blue:** Safety, protection, tranquility, healing
- **Red:** Passion, desire, power, strength, vitality
- **Purple:** Wisdom, spiritual connection, protection

- **Pink:** Peace, emotional support, compassion, affection
- **Black:** Protection, binding, warding off negativity.

You can use a color that resonates with you or when you require the properties associated with it. You can also try to visualize a combination of these colors to design the perfect visual. For example, you should visualize the color purple when cleansing your pendulum and want to remove the stagnant energy. It will also improve your chances of connecting with the spiritual world while performing a divination technique. Similarly, you can visualize the color green when practicing healing rituals. Picture whichever shade of the color resonates best with your intuition and personal preference. The best part about visualization techniques is that there are no strict, set-in-stone rules. You only need to ensure your intentions are right, and the rest will go smoothly.

To perform visualization cleansing of your pendulum, sit in a quiet, comfortable place without distractions. Take a deep breath, hold it for a few seconds, and then exhale. Repeat this twice. Now, visualize white light surrounding you, towering all the way up to the sky. Visualize this light growing more intense and forming a large circle around you.

Now, visualize this light entering your body from your crown chakra and passing through each of the seven chakras, one by one. Finally, imagine this light flowing from your hands to the pendulum that you're holding. Imagine the light engulfing the pendulum and absorbing its negative energy. Then, visualize this light going out of the pendulum and into the ground, where it takes the negative energy to be dissipated. Once you get the hang of this process, cleaning your pendulums with white or any other colored light will only take a few minutes.

7. Crystals

Crystal cleansing is commonly used to dissipate or absorb negative energy from divination objects and tools. Using crystals to remove negative energies from crystal pendulums is the perfect example of using a diamond to cut another diamond. Thanks to the remarkable energy-clearing properties of certain crystals, this method is the most popular for cleansing pendulums. Some crystals that can be used for this process include:

- **Clear Quartz:** This highly effective crystal cleanser is one of the best options for a crystal cleansing ritual. You can keep a clear quartz crystal in the pouch you store the pendulum in – this will ensure that your pendulum stays free of any impure energies from its surroundings.

- **Selenite:** Considered a high vibrational crystal with exceptional cleansing powers, selenite is often used in crystal cleansing techniques. It has a positive energy field that helps protect any object, people, or space around it, freeing it from stagnant negative energy. However, ensure you do not place selenite in water, as it can dissolve very easily. Use a selenite rod to cleanse your pendulum by placing it on top of the crystal. Or, you can opt for a selenite wand and wave it around the pendulum to clear its energy field.

- **Black Obsidian:** A powerful crystal that can be used to remove any negative energy plaguing your pendulum. Add this crystal to your pendulum storage bag to protect the pendulum from inauspicious energies.

8. **Sound**

You'd be surprised to learn that sound cleansing techniques exist to clear away negative energies. Energies can be related to vibrations or frequencies; a sound is also a form of vibration. So, by using different sounds, the vibrations of negative energy can be dissipated from the pendulum. You can use sound tools like crystal bowls, drums, and singing bowls, but also singing, chanting – or even bells. To practice this technique, place the pendulum in a singing bowl and let the vibrations clear the negative energy. Alternatively, place the pendulum on a table and sound the cymbals three times. Make sure you open the windows to let the energy dissipate and avoid trapping it in the room.

Ultimately, the preparation and cleansing of crystals before using them for divination, dowsing, or healing and balancing practices is crucial to the success of the process. However, you can't always control what energies your pendulum absorbs. Both before it gets into your care and after you acquire it, you can effectively get rid of these energies so that these divination tools work properly. Remember that the most important element for cleansing or other processes involving pendulums is the intention set before the process. So, keep positive intentions, and the rest will work out well on its own. Now that you know how to properly cleanse your pendulum, it's time to take a closer look at how to program and charge it for your practice.

Chapter 4: Programming Your Pendulum

Once you've rid your pendulum of any negative energy thanks to cleansing, it's time to program it. Programming your pendulum is just as important as cleansing it. This step ensures that your tool is calibrated and ready to use. While you're probably wondering what the purpose of so many pre-ritual steps is and why you shouldn't jump into pendulum magic rituals directly, keep in mind that without these preliminary steps, you are most likely to get incorrect and off-the-charts readings. So, rather than skip these actions and come up empty-handed, it's best to be prepared. This chapter will provide a detailed guide to programming your pendulum, how to connect with it, and everything else you need to prepare before you can begin using it.

Programming your pendulum is just as important as cleansing it.
https://www.pexels.com/photo/woman-with-silver-pendulum-for-divination-7391631/

Creating a Sacred Space

Before you can program your pendulum, you'll first need to create a safe space for its use. Some people assume creating a safe space for pendulum magic means that negative or evil spirits will be involved, like in Ouija boards or seances. However, pendulum magic involves nothing of the sort. The need for a safe space arises because the space surrounding the pendulum must be cleared of any negative energy, just like the pendulum itself needs to be cleansed.

Understandably, not everyone will be able to designate a specific safe space for pendulum magic, in which case, any space will suffice as long as you cleanse the aura around it before the ritual. To create a safe space, find a small, comfortable spot in your house. This should be a place you're pulled towards and want to use creatively. Whether you designate this space in your bedroom, the lounge, or the study room *is up to you*. Gather things you believe connect to the rituals you plan to perform to add a familiar touch to this space. These can include crystals, wands, shells, figurines, candles, or anything that brings you closer to your pendulum.

Your pendulum kit can also be arranged somewhere in the designated sacred space. Whether you decide to place these items on the floor, a table, a cabinet, or anywhere else is your choice. While decorating this space, let your creative side guide you into finding new ways to decorate the space. Make use of a rug, some fabrics, cushions, and lace cloths to personalize the space. The space doesn't have to be circular in nature or of any general shape.

Most people use their pendulums on a table and sometimes on the floor in front of an altar they've created. Once you've finished decorating the space, take a position at the table or on a cushion on the floor, and observe the energy around the room. If you feel that the room's energy needs cleansing, you can use one of the methods discussed in the previous chapter to shift this energy. For example, if you want to clear the room's energy with smoke, make sure you keep the windows open to let the negative energy go out.

The surrounding energy fields during a pendulum ritual must be completely neutral, free-flowing, and natural. This ensures that any negative energies don't interact with your pendulum and prompt incorrect readings. Before any pendulum reading, you can try the white light visualization activity to further charge this space. To do this, place yourself within the sacred space, sitting or standing, straighten your spine, and close your eyes. Now, visualize a white light surrounding you, growing brighter and stronger until it finally engulfs you and the sacred space, forming a halo of protection around the space.

Then, you can meditate for a few moments before you move on to programming your pendulum for the ritual. To do this, close your eyes and take a few deep breaths. Focus on your breathing, and try to center your brain. Now, direct your intentions for the ritual towards the pendulum. Before meditating, you can light candles or use herbal incense to appease the atmosphere and raise your energy.

Programming Your Pendulum

Once you've created a safe, sacred space, it's time to start programming your pendulum. First, hold the top of the pendulum using your dominant hand's thumb and index finger. There should be a bead or some other small item at the top of the pendulum to hold it. Now, place your elbow on the table, or, if you're sitting on the floor, rest your elbow on your thigh or keep it still and steady. Make sure your wrist stays straight while your elbow remains slightly bent. Your arm should look straight and aligned.

Hold the pendulum with a relaxed grip to ensure there are no restrictions to its movements. Once in a stable, comfortable position, you're now ready to program the pendulum. To do this, you must ensure that the pendulum swings as it is supposed to for yes/no/maybe answers. Although there are no strict rules to follow regarding the pendulum's movement, and the readings depend on your intention and skill, most people prefer to consider the backward and forward movement of the pendulum as "yes." For "no" answers, the pendulum should move sideways or left to right. If the answer to the question is "maybe," the pendulum will move counterclockwise. For a "not now" response, the pendulum will most likely not move, which indicates that now is not the time for this question to be answered. In that case, the procedure should be repeated some other time.

However, these movements aren't the same for every pendulum and every person. This is why programming each pendulum before the ritual is so essential – ensuring its movements align with your considerations and that you do not end up giving wrong readings. The beauty of using a pendulum is that obtaining accurate readings will no longer seem difficult or impossible once you get the hang of its movements. So, before starting any pendulum magic, you must program your pendulum to align with these movements for optimal results.

Connecting with Your Pendulum

Invariably, you'll have to show some patience and get through some important steps before you can start swinging your pendulum and finding answers. Connecting with your pendulum is crucial if you want to get accurate readings, that is, with minimum errors. You must familiarize yourself with how the pendulum swings by practicing, trusting, and focusing on the pendulum. If you pick up the pendulum and start asking questions straight away, you'll get no response, or worse, a completely opposite response to the truth.

So, it's important to keep practicing and getting familiar with the nature of the pendulum. Ideally, you should give your pendulum one week in which you practice using it daily to understand its rhythm and movement. Unlike other divination techniques, you can't simply pick up a card and start interpreting the readings. Pendulum magic requires weeks and months of practice, and when you finally master it, only then will you start getting accurate results. Gradually ease your way into the swinging process of the pendulum, and while focusing on the pendulum, trust yourself, letting go of any expectations, urgency, or intrusive thoughts. Simply let your brain blank out by only focusing on the swing of the pendulum, and let the rest of the process happen naturally.

Aim to set aside fifteen minutes every day during the first week after you program your pendulum to form a connection with it. During this time, sit in your sacred space and simply spend time around your pendulum. You can either meditate, try some yoga, or practice visualization exercises to help establish a connection. This step will prove to be a wonderful experience in your pendulum magic journey while also giving you time to unwind, relax and meditate.

Getting to Know Your Pendulum Exercise

Start this exercise by cleansing yourself, your environment, and your pendulum. You can do this by employing any of the techniques mentioned in the previous chapter. Once you're confident that all negative energies have been cleared away and you feel uplifted and in good spirits, get into a comfortable position within the sacred space. First, you'll need to dissociate from the rest of the world and any problems in your life. Meditation is the best way to achieve this. Practice a meditative sequence that can relax you and help you focus.

You can also decide to use crystals and other spiritual tools during your meditative session. During meditation, concentrate on your breathing and let any other thought leave your mind. Once your mind has cleared and you're in a state of tranquility, take hold of your pendulum and begin to program it. Once you've finished programming it, as explained above, start asking basic questions with yes/no/maybe answers. It is better to ask questions you know the answers to at this early stage instead of queries you're unsure of.

Once you get the hang of how it moves, how long it takes to swing, and if it answers the question correctly, this will help you get to know your pendulum better. During your questioning session, you'll observe that vague questions result in little to no movement of the pendulum, whereas clear questions have an instantaneous response. With that in mind, you must confidently voice your questions using clear, precise wordings. Pendulums swing differently for everyone, so don't despair if your pendulum only swings gently while you've seen others swing great distances.

With time and practice, your pendulum will start to swing as you expect it to. Once you feel enough time has passed and you've started to bond with it, allow the pendulum to move more freely and relax.

Signs That Your Pendulum Works Correctly

The movement of your pendulum depends primarily on your consciousness or subconsciousness. The phrase "Intention is everything" should be considered because it holds true value. While many people consider there to be a universal guide that dictates the movement of pendulums, your subconscious energy actually guides the whole process. For example, suppose you ask your pendulum a question about whether you'll win the lottery. In that case, you're more likely to get an affirmative answer because, subconsciously, that is what you want. The pendulum's clockwise, anticlockwise, sideways, and forward/backward movements are programmed in the same way. You'll cause the pendulum to move in certain directions, and it will, through the invisible energy of your aura.

Once you're properly connected with the pendulum, it will move in the way you tell it to. However, why use it to ask divination questions at all if this is the case? In fact, while pendulums' movement depends on your subconscious energy, once you neutralize your energy, the movement will not be dictated by your desires. Despite that, it can be rather difficult to remain neutral on many topics. For instance, if you ask a question that has emotional significance to you, you'll likely get a biased response from the pendulum due to your energy imbalance. This is why you're advised to meditate and then ask questions calmly and neutrally. Because of this, asking clear questions with simple yes/no answers is best in these readings.

If there's a complex problem you need help with, the best approach is to divide the problem into simpler, yes/no/maybe answer questions and then address them. Once you achieve neutrality and detach yourself from the problem, you're more likely to get an accurate response. Another way you can get viable responses from your pendulum is by using pendulum charts, which will be discussed in detail in an upcoming chapter. These charts will make it easier for you to find answers to your questions.

Storing Your Pendulum

Storing your divination tools is important and should be carried out with great care. Once you've cleansed and programmed your pendulum, you need to store it safely. You'll also need to ensure the crystals on your pendulums are not damaged when kept together. With that in mind, keeping any rough crystals away from tumbled stones is best. Make sure you store them in such a way that they don't scratch each other. If stored carelessly, the surface and luster of the crystal pendulums will be damaged, which may affect the pendulum's movement and overall effectiveness.

If you have a spare jewelry box, you can store each pendulum in a separate compartment of the box. Better yet, you can create a DIY pendulum box. All you need is a box with some compartments; if there are no compartments, you can always add some with a few creative crafts. Another option is to hang them like you would hang necklaces. A necklace holder will make the perfect place to hang your pendulums and keep them in your sacred space.

You should also be careful of your crystal pendulums' chemical and physical compatibility. For example, crystals like selenite and rose quartz are soft in nature and can be easily scratched. Some crystals are also sensitive to water or moisture exposure and will disintegrate if scratched. So, keeping these crystal pendulums safe from moisture and other abrasive materials is crucial. For this purpose, you can wrap them in a soft cloth and store them safely.

Storing each separately for bigger crystal pendulums is essential to ensure they don't damage other crystals. Smaller stones and crystals can be stored in a silk or satin pouch. In order to keep your pendulums pure and effective, always treat them with care and responsibility. When traveling with your pendulums, wrap each one in a separate silk cloth to avoid abrasion. If you don't have access to silk cloths, you can always use eyeglass cloths or even tissue paper to wrap your crystals. Here are other things you should keep in mind:

- Certain crystal types can get faded when kept under direct sunlight. These include citrine, opal, fluorite, aquamarine, topaz, and others. Make sure you practice moon cleansing for these crystal pendulums and store them away from sunlight.
- If you do end up damaging your crystal pendulum, you may still be able to salvage it. If only the surface has been chipped, try to cleanse and program it again. If it shows correct responses, then it's fine. Otherwise, you'll have to replace it.

While pendulum magic is not as complicated as one may imagine it to be, it does have its share of processes and learning. Each process holds a level of importance that cannot be neglected. So, instead of finding shortcuts, it's better to acknowledge the significance of each step and practice them until you perfect them. Programming your pendulum is not something that should be taken lightly. An incorrectly programmed pendulum is as good as a broken one. Make sure to follow and refer back to the guidelines provided in this chapter to have a fully functioning, reliable pendulum.

Chapter 5: Pendulums and Crystals

The popularity of crystals has been growing in the last few years. Something mysterious about their shapes and alluring colors just captures the imagination. However, this isn't the main reason behind their popularity. Crystal healing has become a popular alternative medicine; hence more and more people are curious about these pretty stones. The use of crystals isn't something new. In fact, people have been using crystals throughout history, whether as accessories, home decorations, or to benefit from their healing powers. Nowadays, people still use crystals for the same reasons.

In essence, crystals are minerals that are usually created underground. Each crystal is unique, not just in its shape and color but in its healing properties. Some crystals have peculiar shapes – some are very small, whereas others can be quite large. Crystals can form under various conditions, impacting their shape and color. They come from nature, where they get their energies from the ocean, the moon, or the sun.

Due to their chemical structures, crystals can store energy. Similar to how your brain works, it stays in your memory once you see something. Once a crystal experiences a type of energy, it can carry it forever or until you cleanse it. When you program a crystal by holding it and setting an intention, it will remember and spread this type of energy wherever you place it. For instance, if you set an intention of peace while holding a crystal and place it in your home, it will make your environment more peaceful. Crystals have the power to hold all types of energies, even negative ones, which is why they require cleansing after being exposed to inauspicious energies.

As it happens, crystals don't just spread positive energy around your home. You can place crystals on certain areas of your body to take advantage of their physical, psychological, and emotional benefits. Crystals emit certain vibrations that can interact with your body's energetic frequency – this interaction can create balance in the body to make you feel relaxed and focused. This insightful chapter will delve into the fascinating world of crystals and how you can use them in your pendulum practice.

Crystals and Pendulum Practices

Crystals play a significant role in numerous pendulum practices. You can use their healing abilities against physical ailments to restore your energy or even reconnect with the earth.

Physical and Energy Healing

Crystals can provide healing and protection against various diseases. They act as channels that allow positive and healing energy to flow through your body, pushing out the negative energy causing your ailment. Crystals boast healing properties, and different crystals can help with specific diseases. For example, green aventurine can remedy heart issues. Celestite can alleviate sleeping problems, and amethyst can help people suffering from intestine issues. When someone suffers from a physical condition, the healer should first identify the root cause so they can choose the appropriate crystal to treat their ailment.

Balancing Chakras

As you've seen, your body has seven main energy centers called *chakras*. These centers are responsible for supplying subtle energy to different organs. Each chakra corresponds to one or more of your major organs and nerve bundles and greatly impacts your mental, emotional, spiritual, and physical health. When your chakras are balanced or opened, they allow for the flow of energy throughout your body, keeping you healthy and energetic. However, if any of your chakras are blocked or unbalanced, you'll likely feel your physical and mental health are suffering. Keeping your chakras open is vital to your well-being; this is where crystals come in.

Using crystals is one of the most effective ways to unblock your chakras. Each crystal has unique properties that can connect with the body's energy field and tune into your chakras to restore their balance. Since crystals emit different vibrations, you must use a crystal that has vibrations that target the chakra that requires balancing. There are several crystals associated with each of the seven chakras. Using the right crystal for the blocked chakra will guarantee that the healing process takes place effectively.

The Root Chakra

The root chakra, or Muladhara, is located at the base of the spine. It is responsible for making you feel secure and safe. When this chakra is out of balance, you may suffer from hip or lower back issues and experience anxiety and depression. The best crystals for balancing the root chakra should be dark and have protective and grounding properties. This chakra is also associated with the colors red, silver, brown, and black, so opt for crystals of those colors, including:

- Black Tourmaline
- Obsidian
- Smoke Quartz
- Bloodstone
- Red Jasper
- Mystical Merlinite

The Sacral Chakra

The sacral chakra, or Swadhisthana, is located in the lower abdomen. It is associated with sexuality and creativity. When this chakra is out of balance, you may experience issues with your libido and struggle with sexual expression and pleasure. The best crystals to use for this chakra are orange since this color is most associated with the sacral chakra. Some include:

- Carnelian
- Orange calcite
- Orange jasper
- Sunstone
- Peach moonstone

Solar Plexus Chakra

The solar plexus chakra, or Manipura, is located around the navel area. This chakra is responsible for your willpower and self-worth. You may become angry, controlling, and powerless when it's unbalanced. You may also experience physical symptoms like indigestion. Yellow and gold crystals are ideal for bringing balance to the solar plexus chakra and can include the following:

- Yellow jasper
- Tiger's eye
- Citrine
- Pyrite

The Heart Chakra

The heart chakra, or Anahata, is located in the center of the chest. Unsurprisingly, this energy center is responsible for all matters related to romance, compassion, and empathy. When this chakra is out of balance, you may not be able to feel empathy or connect with others and may struggle with letting go of grudges. Green but also pink crystals will open up your blocked heart chakra. These include:

- Rhodochrosite
- Rose Quartz
- Malachite
- Jade
- Emerald
- Jade
- Peach Moonstone

The Throat Chakra

The throat chakra, or Vishuddha, is located in the throat area. It is responsible for communication, speaking, and self-expression. When this chakra is unbalanced, you may lie and gossip, feel confused, and be left unable to express yourself. Blue crystals are your best option for bringing balance to the throat chakra, including:

- Blue Kyanite
- Blue Apatite
- Lapis Lazuli

- Amazonite
- Sodalite
- Aquamarine

Third Eye Chakra

The third eye chakra, or Ajna, is located right between the eyebrows. It is responsible for dreams and imagination. When this chakra is out of balance, you may feel that your thoughts are out of control and experience brain fog and delusions. Indigo and violet crystals will help with unblocking the third eye chakra. These include:

- Lepidolite
- Lapis lazuli
- Amethyst
- Labradorite

The Crown Chakra

The crown chakra, or Sahasrara, is the last of the seven chakras. Located at the top of the head, this chakra is responsible for connecting you with the universe and finding your purpose. When unbalanced, you may not be enthusiastic about your future and lose your sense of purpose. When it comes to unblocking the crown chakra, stick to white and violet crystals, such as:

- Moonstone
- Selenite
- Celestite
- Crystal Quartz
- Golden Heart

Grounding

Another pendulum practice where crystals can be effective is grounding. Grounding allows you to connect with the energy of the earth. It enables you to be calm, collected, centered, and balanced, especially during times of turmoil. Feeling grounded is associated with being true to yourself and clear thinking to make good life decisions. If you feel that you're losing your connection with the earth and life has made you unsettled, crystals can ground you and help you rekindle your balance. They will allow you to connect with the earth's energy, wisdom, and everything it offers.

There are specific crystals that are powerful enough to bring stability and strength back into your life. These will help you live in the present moment without worrying over the past or concerning yourself with the future. They can also help you let go of any negative energy affecting your spirit, body, and mind. Grounding crystals can also provide protection and prevent toxic energy from disturbing your inner peace. This section will go over some of the most effective crystals for grounding.

Hematite

Hematite is a powerful crystal that can ground you and reconnect you with the earth. It will restore your balance while releasing negative emotions like anxiety and insecurity. Hematite can also rebalance your root chakra, which is responsible for your sense of stability. That way, you'll allow the energy to flow through your body to make you feel grounded.

Hematite can rebalance your root chakra.
Stephanie Clifford from Arlington, VA, USA, CC BY 2.0 <https://creativecommons.org/licenses/by/2.0>, via Wikimedia Commons: https://commons.wikimedia.org/wiki/File:Hematite_(3561496162).jpg

As mentioned, many grounding crystals also provide protection, and hematite is one of them. It will protect you against negative energy threatening your stability and balance. This dynamic crystal acts like a magnet that pulls you down to earth.

Smoky Quartz

Another powerful grounding crystal is smoky quartz. It can rid you of negative emotions like restlessness, stress, and fear. Once these emotions are released, you'll experience feelings of clarity, calmness, and grounding. Smoky quartz replaces emotions that don't serve you with positive ones that will benefit your spirit, mind, and body. For instance, if you are prone to anxiety, this crystal can help you put these feelings into perspective and work through them instead of letting them disturb your peace.

Smoky quartz replaces emotions that don't serve you with positive ones.
Ra'ike (see also: de:Benutzer:Ra'ike), CC BY-SA 3.0 <https://creativecommons.org/licenses/by-sa/3.0>, via Wikimedia Commons: https://commons.wikimedia.org/wiki/File:Quartz_-_Smoky_quartz_from_Obersulzbachtal_-_Austria.jpg

Smoky quartz can be a better option for some people compared to hematite. Hematite's energy is so powerful that it can feel overwhelming, which is typically not the case for smoky quartz, thanks to its more subtle kind of energy.

Black Tourmaline

Black Tourmaline is associated with the root chakra.
https://pixabay.com/es/photos/turmalina-negra-muestra-roca-rock-1609432/

Black tourmaline acts as a protective stone against negative energy. It is also associated with the root chakra, which, when balanced, can provide grounding and stability. This crystal can also boost your confidence, increase your strength, and make you feel steady. Black tourmaline can connect you with nature so you can feel safe and secure, releasing feelings like anxiety and fear in the process.

Jasper

It isn't uncommon for a person to lose their way in life. Luckily, jasper can help you reconnect with the Earth and find your way back to yourself, especially during times of uncertainty. This crystal can bring you balance and stability while providing you with determination, strength, and courage. When you feel exhausted or overwhelmed in your everyday life, the jasper crystal can reenergize you and refresh your body and mind. It can also bolster your creativity whenever you feel stuck or uninspired.

Jasper can help you reconnect with the Earth.
https://pixabay.com/es/photos/piedras-rocas-jaspe-jaspe-rojo-7182407/

People have been using jasper for centuries for its grounding and healing properties. This crystal contains powerful earth energy that can strengthen your bond with the earth. While there are several types of jasper stones with different shades, they all have strong earth energy inside of them.

Obsidian

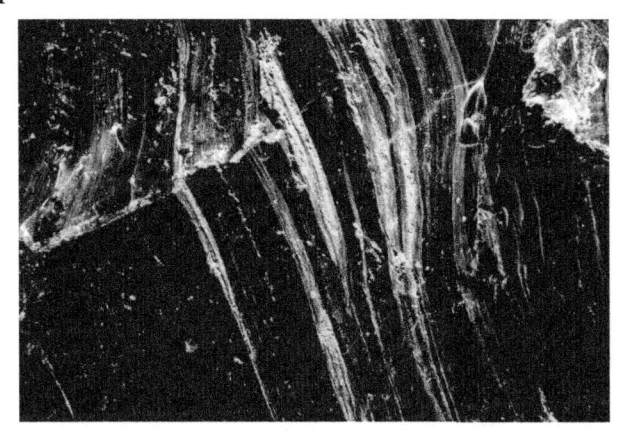

Obsidian acts as a shield to protect you against negative emotions.
https://www.pexels.com/photo/close-up-of-obsidian-4766367/

Obsidian has remarkable grounding properties that can balance and stabilize your spirit, mind, and body. It isn't rare for people to suppress certain negative emotions, which can directly impact their mental and physical health. Obsidian can help you become aware of these feelings so you can confront them instead of running away from them. It also acts as a shield to protect you against negative emotions.

Onyx

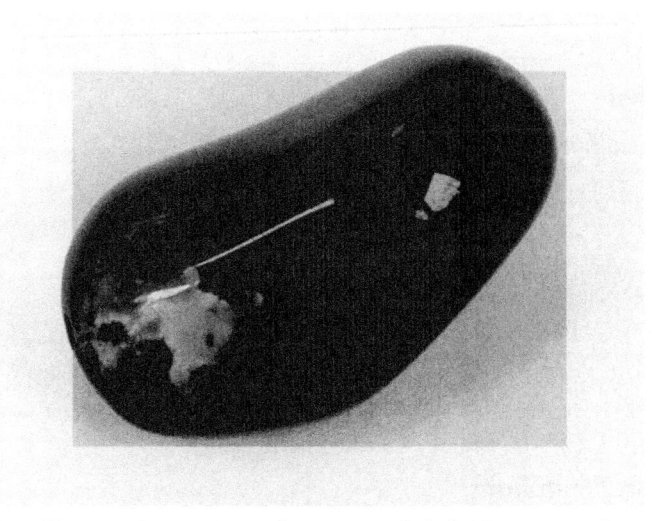

Onyx provides guidance and reassurance whenever you feel afraid or unsure about your future.
Simon Eugster --Simon 14:41, 11 April 2006 (UTC), CC BY-SA 3.0
<http://creativecommons.org/licenses/by-sa/3.0/>, via Wikimedia Commons:
https://commons.wikimedia.org/wiki/File:Onyx.jpg

Not only is onyx a grounding stone, but it can also release stress and bring balance and harmony back into your life. Whenever you experience fear, onyx has the power to support you until you can get rid of these feelings for good. Various negative emotions often accompany anxiety, worry, and stress. This crystal can eliminate these feelings and replace them with positive ones. If you ever feel out of your comfort zone, onyx can help you through these situations. This crystal will also provide guidance and reassurance whenever you feel afraid or unsure about your future. The onyx crystal is associated with several chakras: the third eye chakra, the root chakra, the crown chakra, and the solar plexus chakra.

Types of Crystal Pendulums

Chakras Healing Pendulums

The first type of crystal pendulum is the chakra healing pendulum. A crystal pendulum can unblock your chakras to improve your emotional, spiritual, mental, and physical health. By using this method, you'll be able to determine the energy level in each chakra to see which ones require balancing, so you can begin the healing process. The best tool for this method is the seven-chakra pendulum, as it features all the main crystals of the seven chakras:

- Amethyst
- Red jasper
- Iolite
- Carnelian
- Lapis lazuli
- Green aventurine
- Golden calcite

You can use this type of pendulum to communicate with your higher self and spirit guides and ask them any questions on your mind. This pendulum is ideal for people working with chakras and looking to bring balance to any or all of the seven chakras.

Divination Pendulums

Various crystals can be used for divination purposes. This type of pendulum can raise your higher spiritual energy and protect you from negative vibes. Crystals known to intensify and transform your energy include quartz of various shades.

Healing Crystals

As established, crystals have strong healing properties. If you plan to start working with crystal pendulums, it's good to be aware of the most common crystals and learn about how they can help you. These include:

Angelite

Angelite can provide guidance and help you work with your higher self.
Didier Descouens, CC BY-SA 3.0 <https://creativecommons.org/licenses/by-sa/3.0>, via Wikimedia Commons: https://commons.wikimedia.org/wiki/File:Anhydrite_Arnave.jpg

Angelite is one of the most popularly used crystals in pendulums. It is suitable for divination and spiritual work, as it can help you connect with your spiritual guides. This light blue crystal can also provide guidance and help you work with your higher self.

Rose Quartz

Rose Quartz can help restore balance to the heart chakra.
https://www.pexels.com/photo/rose-quartz-crystals-on-glass-surface-4391421/

Rose quartz is a favorite among many people, especially those who seek healing for matters of the heart. This crystal can help restore balance to the heart chakra. The rose quartz is ideal for people struggling with forgiveness, as it can help them let go of the past so they can forgive others and, most of all, forgive themselves. It can also help you love and accept yourself for who you are and happily receive love from others. This crystal emits vibrations of unconditional love and heals the body, mind, and spirit by bringing you harmony and balance.

Clear Quartz

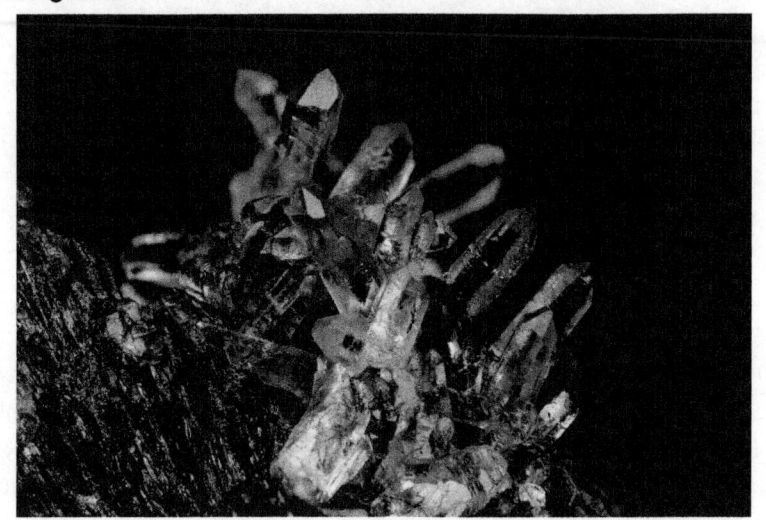

Clear quartz can provide clarity to the mind.
https://www.pexels.com/photo/a-cluster-of-quartz-crystal-9037438/

Clear quartz is perhaps the most popular healing crystal, and for a good reason. It is often referred to as "the master healer." Clear quartz can bring balance to any of your seven chakras and provide clarity to the mind. It can also attune to the energies of any other crystal. Another advantage to this crystal is that you can easily program it to access a higher state of consciousness. You can also use this crystal in various rituals, including grounding and self-healing.

Kunzite

Kunzite will provide you with an abundance of love and compassion.
Didier Descouens, CC BY-SA 4.0 <https://creativecommons.org/licenses/by-sa/4.0>, via Wikimedia Commons: https://commons.wikimedia.org/wiki/File:Kunzite_Nouristan.jpg

No one can live without love and compassion. If you find your life lacking these two emotions, give kunzite a chance. It will provide you with an abundance of love and compassion. This crystal has various healing properties, helping you heal from past relationships, cleanse your aura, and open your heart to the love and acceptance of those around you. Thanks to its grounding and calming properties, kunzite can also help bring harmony into your life.

Citrine

Citrine can help you release negative energy and replace it with positivity.
https://pixabay.com/es/photos/citrino-gemas-cristal-brillante-7433765/

Everyone needs a little sunshine and positivity in their lives. This yellow, sun-shaded crystal can impart positive vibrations into your life, making you grateful and more appreciative of everything you have. Citrine can help you release negative energy and replace it with positivity. It promotes growth and pushes you to achieve your goals with a positive attitude. This crystal is associated with the solar plexus chakra and can restore its balance.

Malachite

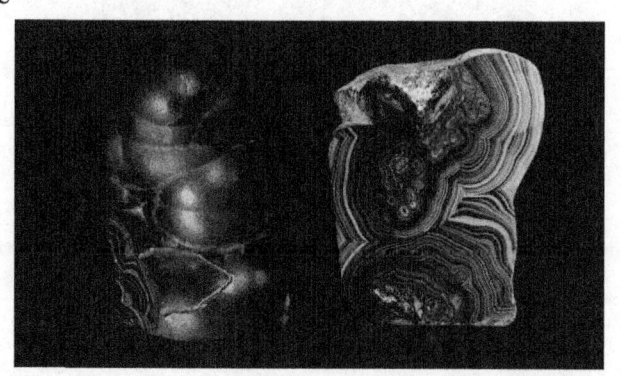

Malachite can offer deep healing, protection, and energetic support.
Didier Descouens, CC BY-SA 3.0 <https://creativecommons.org/licenses/by-sa/3.0>, via Wikimedia Commons:
https://commons.wikimedia.org/wiki/File:Malachite_Kolwezi_Katanga_Congo.jpg

Malachite is the crystal of bravery, providing you with courage and strength. Suppose your life abounds with uncertainty and fear, especially regarding money. In that case, this crystal can offer deep healing, protection, and energetic support. Whatever pain, wounds, or old trauma you have experienced in your life, malachite will help you overcome these emotions and move on from loss and heartache.

Moonstone

Moonstone can enrich your life with positive feelings.
Gemsphoto, CC BY-SA 4.0 <https://creativecommons.org/licenses/by-sa/4.0>, via Wikimedia Commons:
https://commons.wikimedia.org/wiki/File:Natural_Blue_Moonstone_loose_gemstone.jpg

Moonstone has several healing properties. It can help you remain focused, provides support, and helps you balance your emotions. It can also help you establish a deep connection with the divine feminine. Moonstone can enrich your life with positive feelings like acceptance, curiosity, patience, acceptance, and nurturing.

Lepidolite

Lepidolite can provide a sense of calmness to your nervous system.
© Zbynek Burival / Mineralexpert.org:
https://commons.wikimedia.org/wiki/File:Lepidolite_from_Rozna_Czech_Republic.jpg

Lepidolite calms and relaxes the body and mind. If your emotions are boiling, your body is tense, and your mind is stressed, this crystal can help soothe all these intense feelings. Lepidolite can provide a sense of calmness to your nervous system and help people suffering from anxiety, insomnia, or panic disorder.

Black Tourmaline

Black tourmaline can help release underlying negative emotions.
Texas Lane, CC BY-SA 4.0 <https://creativecommons.org/licenses/by-sa/4.0>, via Wikimedia Commons: https://commons.wikimedia.org/wiki/File:Raw_Black_Tourmaline.jpg

When negative energy flows through your body, it affects your well-being and consumes you, and leaves no room for positivity. Black tourmaline can help release underlying negative emotions and free up space for positive energy. This crystal also acts as a powerful protective stone that can shield you from external negative energy.

Amethyst

Amethyst has physical, emotional, and spiritual healing properties.
https://www.pexels.com/photo/set-of-shiny-transparent-amethysts-grown-together-4040567/

Derived from the Greek "amethystos," the word amethyst means "not intoxicated." The ancient Greeks believed this crystal to hold protective powers that could protect people from the effects of intoxication from alcohol. In fact, the ancient Egyptians, Romans, and Greeks all harnessed the healing powers of this crystal. It has a characteristic glassy luster and comes in eye-catching shades of purple and violet. Amethyst is considered a bridge that connects the physical and the divine world. It has always been associated with spirituality and spiritual healing and is known to bring back balance to the crown chakra and third eye chakra. Amethyst has physical, emotional, and spiritual healing properties. It can keep you calm, help you to make better decisions, balance your emotions, give you courage, boost your immune system, heal migraines, and reduce negative energy.

Selenite

Selenite can heal the body and mind.
Bryan Barnes, CC BY-SA 4.0 <https://creativecommons.org/licenses/by-sa/4.0>, via Wikimedia Commons: https://commons.wikimedia.org/wiki/File:NM_Selenite_Crystal_Cluster.jpg

Selenite is associated with consciousness and clarity, and people often refer to it as the "goddess stone." Selenite is derived from Selene, the Greek goddess of the moon, who was a powerful deity that could bring light to the darkest of nights. Thanks to its name and association with the Greek goddess, Selenite is considered one of the most spiritual crystals in the world. Its color is often compared to angel wings, which adds to its mysticism. It is known for its soothing properties and can bring harmony and protection. Selenite can heal the body and mind, helping to realign the skeleton, manage anxiety, and bring balance to the heart chakra.

How to Choose a Crystal Pendulum

One of the first things people do before choosing a crystal is checked out its description. However, this information isn't always comprehensive or helpful. Each person will have a unique experience with the crystals they use. The information you read only shows one aspect of what the crystals offer. This doesn't mean you should ignore this information, as it can give you an idea of what each crystal can do. Don't rely on it completely when making a decision.

Do you choose a crystal, or does the crystal choose you? Select the crystals that speak to you and those you feel most drawn to or connected with. While choosing a crystal purely based on shape and color is tempting, you're looking for something much deeper and more personal. Hold different crystals in your hand and try to identify what you are feeling. Pick the crystal that you experience an energetic connection with.

To narrow down your options and better understand what to look for, identify your issues so you can select the stone with the appropriate healing properties. Make sure you follow your intuition and look for a connection.

Crystals have been around for thousands of years, and many people have used them for their numerous beneficial properties. Today, people wear crystals or place them around their homes to reap their natural benefits. Crystals have become a part of various pendulum practices, as they provide healing properties and can bring balance to the seven chakras. Whether it's divination, balancing chakras, or grounding, you can always count on crystals to satisfy your spiritual needs.

Chapter 6: Pendulums for Dowsing and Divination

This chapter discusses what it takes to develop your skills for pendulum dowsing and divination. Before that, you'll learn what divination is and what it isn't. You'll get to delve much deeper into these two terms, laying the foundation for a successful practice. Last, but not least, you'll discover how intuition is linked to divination – something you'll read more about later in the book.

Pendulum dowsing is one of the earliest recorded methods of divination.
https://pixabay.com/es/photos/p%c3%a9ndulo-la-radiestesia-espiritual-4868645/

What Is Divination?

Divination can be defined in many ways, with the most common description being the art of predicting the future. However, while divination methods can reveal certain aspects of the future, they're not fortune-telling. No divination method will provide precise answers about your future because you're constantly shaping it with your behavior. Even the smallest thought can lead to behavior that changes the course of your life and affect the future. For that reason, divination should only be viewed as a tool to gain insight into events, situations, or questions about a person's life. This insight is the potential outcome of the behavior dictated by the thoughts in your subconscious mind. Divinatory tools help tap into these thoughts and access information that otherwise wouldn't be accessible. The subconscious part of your mind stores this information as ingrained thought patterns. Divinatory tools can help you translate these into images or other stimuli that you can perceive with the conscious part of your mind. Apart from your subconscious mind, the information can also come from other higher beings, such as ancestral souls and spiritual guides.

Several forms of divination include dream interpretation, tarot card divination, runecasting, reading tea leaves, scrying, crystal ball divination, pendulum dowsing, and other techniques. As with any other method, pendulum dowsing requires you to learn how to interpret messages – which is only possible if you're able to tap into your intuition. After all, you're gaining a higher knowledge only your higher self can decipher. The best way to reach your higher self is by tapping into your gut. Why? Because dowsing (and divination itself) is a form of communication in which you rely on energy. You're connecting your intuitive power with the life forms around you, so you can interpret the messages you receive. Whether you seek knowledge and assistance from your spiritual guides or simply want to communicate with them, you'll need your intuition to get the message through.

Divination is an ancient form of predicting the future, and pendulum dowsing is one of the earliest recorded methods. Its simplicity makes it the ideal tool for beginners, as pendulums are easy to make, use, and maintain between sessions. As explained earlier, the questions posed during pendulum divinatory dowsing practices are also straightforward, with simple "yes" or "no" answers. As long as the questions are specific enough, you can find plenty of information in these simple answers. That said, dowsing only entails confirming the information you already have in your subconscious. You're not foreseeing new facts. There are several ways to apply this to divination, and you can tailor the methods to your liking.

Now, before embarking on your dowsing journey, you'll need to decide the reasons for starting it. Despite popular belief, simply wanting to know your future isn't a good enough cause. For your reason to be compelling, it needs to be realistic and formulated in a way that helps you grow. Remember, you're the creator of your own reality. You're the only one who knows how to shape your future the way you want it to look. You can manifest a future outcome, but you'll also be able to work for it. So, after receiving a message about a future event, you'll need to analyze it and see what you can do to make it come to life. Divination is one of the purest and most accurate forms of understanding the future. That said, it takes serious and consistent practice until you master this art.

Pendulum Dowsing in Detail

First and foremost, you must consider your pendulum as an extension of your intuitive energy. The type of tools you use for dowsing always depends on what feels right for you at the moment. Whether you buy a pendulum or create one on your own, it only matters that you can connect it to your intuition – and yes, your gut will let you know whether you have the right tool. Crystals are the most common choice for pendulum dowsing. Some popular crystals used for dowsing include:

- **Amethyst:** Often associated with the spiritual world.
- **Clear Quartz:** Linked to mental clarity and the connection to a higher purpose.
- **Rose Quartz:** Popular for grounding and calming the senses before dowsing rituals.

Since different occasions may require different energies, you can have several pendulums for dowsing. For beginners, choosing only one pendulum and practicing your dowsing and divination skills with it is recommended. Once you get the hang of interpreting simple messages, you'll be able to upgrade to more complex practices.

Before you start using your pendulum, you should always prepare it (cleansing and charging it with your energy, as described in the previous chapters). This is a crucial step for making it work with your intuition.

Whichever method you choose to ensure the tools are enveloped only in your positive and intentional energy, make sure you take enough time to do it properly. You can check whether the pendulum is connected to your energy field before each session by spending 5-10 minutes sitting with it in your hands. Keep your eyes closed, breathe steadily, and just feel the energy going back and forth in your arm.

Some practitioners prefer to say a prayer or make an offering to their guides before beginning the divination. If you're working with a guide, this is also the best time to reach out to them. In case your preparation takes more than 15 minutes, you should consider taking out your pendulum only a minute or two before you're ready to use it. This will help you keep it safe and away from any source of negative energy so it remains a faithful extension of your intuition.

How to Get Started with Pendulum Dowsing

There are two fundamental principles in pendulum dowsing and divination itself. One is keeping an open mind, and the other is setting aside any judgment or preconceived notion you may have about the practice. As mentioned before, you won't get precise answers such as names, dates, or specific situations. So, to get the most accurate results possible, you'll need to keep an open mind about the messages you receive about the future. It's also possible to get several different answers for the same question or one answer that doesn't tell you anything about what you are interested in. This often happens to novices and only means you'll need to practice a bit more. However, the more open you are to the possibilities in the beginning, the easier you'll learn to interpret the messages. New practitioners often get stuck trying to decipher the information about the future simply because they focus on the answer already in their minds. You may assume you know the answer, but this isn't necessarily true. And the sooner you accept that the answer may differ from what you expect, the sooner you can get aligned with your future path.

Another mistake many novices make is expecting the pendulum to start swinging in clear directions right away. This rarely happens because your reflexes aren't yet in tune with the pendulum – even if your energy is. The pendulum must be under the influence of your reflexes for a while before it starts behaving as you would expect it. Maintain focus even if you don't feel you'll receive anything during the session. Keep your mind on your intention, but don't force it in the direction of any particular answer, as this could give you a false view of potential future outcomes.

Using your dominant hand to hold the pendulum when dowsing is a great way to get it aligned with your intuition. If you don't know which hand is your dominant hand, hold the pendulum in the one that feels more comfortable. You can try out both and see what your intuition tells you about which hand the pendulum feels closer to your higher being. The same goes for the length of the pendulum. To keep it close to you, use a shorter cord or chain, or simply wrap the excess around your forefinger. When you have prepared your mind, body, and space and brought your question into your focus, you can start dowsing using the following steps:

1. Sit in a comfortable position, and hold the pendulum between your index and thumb. Trace the length of the cord or chain with your other hand, stopping at the bottom of it with your palm facing upward.
2. Wait until the pendulum becomes still before moving your hand away from under it. If it starts moving again, don't worry, as this is entirely normal.
3. Relax your body by moving your shoulders back and straightening your spine. This also promotes energy flow through your body, making the messages more transparent.
4. Sit and watch the pendulum move until it stops again.
5. Now, you can start determining the proper responses you expect about what you're dowsing for.
6. Ask the pendulum a question you already know has a "yes" answer, and see how it moves. You can affirm this by repeatedly asking it to show you a "yes" message.
7. Repeat the same with a question that has a "no" for an answer. The question should be related to answers you can clearly see without the need for dowsing. For example, if it's a Saturday, you can ask whether the next day will be Sunday.
8. If you still can't tell the difference between the responses, or if the pendulum changes the movement even with the same response, repeat the entire process as many times as necessary.
9. Once you've learned how to distinguish clearly between the "yes" and "no" answers, you'll be ready to ask more informative

questions that can be answered with these. For example, you can ask the pendulum whether you'll find the item you want to buy on your next shopping trip.

It takes time to learn how to dowse confidently and find every bit of information you're looking for. As your confidence grows, you'll be able to ask more personal questions because you'll know that your intuition will always give you a reliable answer. You can also try specific exercises such as locating missing objects, pets, or places you've never been before. Just as the explorers dowse for water and precious metals in the future, so can you for exploring new areas near you. You'll need a simple map and hold the pendulum over it. After asking the questions, you observe the pendulum moving over specific parts of the map.

Practicing Divination with a Pendulum

This simple yet effective technique will help you understand your intuition and gain access to your subconscious thoughts. It will enable you to use your pendulum for divination. Here is how to do it:

1. Sit or stand in a comfortable position with your shoulders and body relaxed. There should be no tension in your arms or legs, either.
2. Place your hand palm up on a table, altar, or other sacred space in front of you, and take several deep breaths.
3. Take your time to relax, and perform breathing exercises, meditation, or other grounding techniques.
4. When you feel relaxed enough, ask the pendulum to show an affirmative answer in the same way as described in the dowsing section. Learning how to dowse is recommended first, as it helps you understand and calibrate the responses.
5. Wait until the pendulum starts moving, and you get a "yes" for an answer.
6. Repeat the process for the "no" answer by asking the pendulum for it.
7. You can now start asking simple yet specific questions. These may also serve you as a practice but can sometimes deliver a meaningful message.
8. You'll apply the same principle as you did with the dowsing techniques. The only exception is that all the questions (the

practice and the main ones) should pertain to future outcomes and not something you want to find.

9. Finally, you should begin using the pendulum to gain insight into questions about the future. Again, start with a simple question. For example, you can ask whether it's a good idea to wear a particular outfit the next day. If the weather is expected to change, you'll probably get a negative answer.

10. As you practice this technique, you'll eventually learn to get answers to even more substantial questions – such as whether you should change jobs, relocate, continue your studies, and more.

Techniques and Tips for Developing Dowsing and Divination Skills

To get the best results and avoid misusing your pendulum, you should only use it when your mind frame is apt for dowsing or divination. Your emotions should be balanced and your thoughts controlled. It's a good idea to do a mental health check from time to time to ensure you remain motivated to keep honing your pendulum-wielding skills. If you aren't sure whether you're ready to use your pendulum, ask it. The tool will connect to your intuition and tell you right away if something is wrong.

While dowsing can be used to uncover potential health issues, including allergies, it should never replace a consultation with a medical professional. If you have a health concern, you should seek medical assistance as soon as possible. It's also a good idea to avoid dowsing for other people's health issues in the beginning. Once you can assert that you're skilled enough to perform this task, you may go ahead but only do it after gaining the other person's approval. You can use the pendulum to seek answers about someone else's future, but only if you have their permission. Be sure to explain to them the importance of keeping an open mind, as this will be necessary to align their energy with the pendulum and obtain an accurate reading.

Both pendulum dowsing and divination have limitations, which you and whomever your target should be aware of. Sometimes, it may be a good idea to consult other divination forms, especially if you're interested in learning how the past and present affect the future. However, pendulums will be the right way to go if you're only interested in clear affirmative or dissentient responses. That said, you shouldn't rely on pendulum dowsing to make decisions all the time. While you can use it to facilitate decision-making, it should never be your only driving force. Take responsibility for your actions, and start creating your own reality. Most importantly, if you change your behavior and the outcomes change, don't blame it on your tool if the newest development isn't to your liking.

What Can Affect Your Results?

Several factors may affect the results of pendulum dowsing and divination. Here are the most common ones:

The Force of Movement

The first and perhaps most decisive factor is the force your reflexes use to move the pendulum. This determines how forcefully the tool will move. For example, a strong swing in a predetermined direction (calibrated with the "yes" and "no" answers) signals a strong possibility of the message representing the truth. These types of responses are typically more reliable than the light swing in either direction. If the pendulum barely moves, this typically means the tool can't commit to giving you the answers. With dowsing, this can be caused by numerous factors. Meanwhile, a non-committal answer in divination usually means the outcome hasn't been determined yet.

Interpreting the Answers

Your ability to interpret the answers may also affect your capacity to find the answers you seek. Here is a great technique to practice if you want to see the answers more clearly:

1. Prepare your mind and focus it on the questions you need answers to.
2. Hold the pendulum in one hand and see how it swings while focusing on the questions even more intently.
3. Wait until the pendulum registers your energy. The time for this to happen varies. Sometimes, you'll get a quick response, while you need to wait a few minutes at other times. Be prepared for either possibility.
4. Think about how the pendulum signaled the response during the practice sessions or the previous time you used it for dowsing or divination.
5. Once you have your response, take your time to interpret it.

6. If you're uncertain whether you've got the correct response or seen it appropriately, ask another question from the pendulum. The more questions you ask, the better insight you'll gain into your topic of interest.

Relaxation

Your ability to relax is another essential aspect you may need to work on. While the steady rocking motion of the pendulum is designed to help you focus during the session, it doesn't always work perfectly. Sometimes, it excites the body so much that you simply lose focus on the task ahead. For maximum efficacy, you should be in a calm and neutral state of mind, which may require some work. Once that's achieved, the swaying or spinning motion of the pendulum will work wonders on seeping into your subconscious and accessing your intuitive wisdom.

Possible Issues with Pendulum Dowsing and Divination

There could be several reasons your pendulum may not offer accurate results when dowsing or looking into the future. Here are some of them:

- You haven't learned the proper language of your pendulum. Try practicing the "yes" and "no" responses again.
- You're too stressed to focus on your question or interpret the results correctly. Calm down before trying again.
- You have negative feelings or doubts about future outcomes even before seeing them. Make sure you dissipate these before interpreting the results.
- You may have electrical equipment disrupting the flow of energy around the pendulum. Use pendulums away from all gadgets and machines.
- Your pendulum hasn't been properly cleansed, charged, or programmed.
- Your questions aren't simple or specific enough, so you'll need to reformulate them.
- You haven't waited enough time. It may take more time for the question to reach its destination. Make sure you wait enough time for the answer to manifest itself.

- Your pendulum may not be aligned with your energy. Try finding a different one to see whether its energy is a better fit.

Chapter 7: Create a Pendulum Chart

When you hear the word pendulum, an image of a small sphere attached to a string, swaying left to right, landing on either "yes" or "no," comes to mind. Pendulum charts, however, extend the abilities of pendulums. They allow you to receive more complex answers than just "yes," "no," or "maybe." While using pendulum charts requires relatively more advanced skills, they can easily be learned with knowledge and practice.

Using a pendulum chart that suits your needs increases your likelihood of retrieving relevant information and guidance.
https://pixabay.com/es/photos/p%c3%a9ndulo-paneles-de-p%c3%a9ndulo-tablero-242740/

There are numerous types of pendulum charts, some more complex than others. While they may look different, they all operate in the same way. Yes or no pendulum charts use pre-programmed symbols. In other words, the chart has reference points that the pendulum uses to reveal the answers to your questions.

Using a pendulum chart that suits your needs increases your likelihood of retrieving relevant information and receiving guidance. Using the right pendulum chart allows you to ask more specific and detailed questions about several broader aspects of life. Suppose you use a pendulum chart that encompasses many possibilities. In that case, you can end up with information that you didn't even ask for in the first place. This is why people who have experience using pendulum charts are able to communicate more effectively with the divine.

Luckily, you can make pendulum charts at home easily. All you need is basic guidance and some common household materials. You need to follow very few rules when making a pendulum chart. Primarily, you'll have to rely on your intuition and imagination to come up with formats and keywords that will answer the questions that you have in mind.

This chapter covers everything you need to know about using and creating pendulum charts. You'll find out how to prepare yourself before working with a pendulum chart to ensure a fruitful experience. You'll also learn about the different types of pendulum charts and how to create and work with each one.

Before You Start

Before we can delve into making and using pendulum charts, you must find out how to prepare yourself for this process.

Center Yourself

Centering yourself before working with a pendulum chart is essential. Otherwise, you won't receive answers to the questions you direct at the pendulum. This is because you don't receive answers from the pendulum itself. It's an inanimate object, which is why your subconscious mind will not comprehend how or why you're trying to obtain answers from an object that lacks consciousness.

When working with a pendulum, you must instead direct your question to your higher self. Centering yourself allows you to shift your focus toward this intention. Start by finding a quiet place where you can work without any distractions. It's best to dedicate a space or corner of your home to divination practices, as we've explained in a previous chapter. This can be the spot that you always turn to whenever you need to center yourself. Make it as comfortable as you desire. You can use a mat, light up a few candles, or even place a comfortable chair and coffee table.

It also helps to burn incense or diffuse relaxing essential oils. That said, make sure that the decor and lighting aren't too stimulating for the senses. Tailoring the environment to your needs allows you to feel calm and at peace and encourages you to use it for other soothing purposes, such as meditating or reading.

Shift your focus to your breathing, keeping it as slow and steady as possible. Draw in deep breaths, releasing all the tension from your body as you exhale. Visualize the worry, stress, and anxiety exiting your body with each breath you take. Keep your focus there for a few minutes before moving on to meditation techniques.

Choose any meditation practice that you feel comfortable working with. Many people like to use the chakra harmonizing visualization technique, where you picture a white light engulfing you. You can also go for any simple breathing exercise that allows you to enter a relaxed state.

Come up with "Yes" or "No" Questions

Now that you feel appeased and grounded, think of the questions you wish to ask. Make sure they're focused, concise, simple, and clear. Start with questions that only require "yes" or "no" answers. Write down all the questions you want to ask on a piece of paper and test the pendulum before moving on to more complex charts. Make sure to include some questions to which you already know the answer, such as "Am I a woman?" "Is tomorrow Sunday?" and "Do I live with my parents?"

Reframe Your Thoughts

It's normal to feel confused when you're still learning to use the pendulum. You may experience difficulty getting your pendulum to move and give you an answer. Even if it does, you may doubt the response and wonder if it was a mere coincidence. Some people worry that their ego is what prompts the movement of the pendulum rather than their higher self. Others experience no difficulties getting the pendulum to swing right away. Ultimately, your ability to receive a response is directly associated with your headspace. This is why saying positive affirmations can help you get rid of any beliefs and preconceived notions that may be holding you back. Reframing your thoughts and maintaining a positive mindset are essential when practicing divination techniques.

Practicing the following steps will help you avoid any troubles throughout the process:

Step 1: Visualization

Start visualizing a large ball of light on top of your head. The bright, golden-white light is a symbol of your higher self and your superconscious mind. Imagine it growing larger, connecting your crown chakra and your third eye to your head.

Step 2: Recite Releasing Statements

This isn't just about repeating them loudly. You have to believe in what you're saying. To do that, stand in a private space, speak slowly and articulately, and take the time to savor and feel your words as if they were really happening. Maintain a positive mindset throughout the process.

Releasing statements can help you get rid of any limiting beliefs. They allow you to let go of those fears that you hold deep within your subconscious mind. These convictions and worries block you from moving forward and prevent you from learning the truth from your spirit guides and higher self.

The following are some releasing statements that you can recite:

- I allow myself to let go of all judgment, perception, and conviction that I am fearful of working with my higher self and superconscious mind to unlock the truth.
- I choose to get rid of the need to believe that I am afraid to work with my higher self and superconscious mind.
- I release all judgment, perception, and conviction that learning the truth will harm me and others.
- I release all judgment, perception, and conviction that I am anxious about learning the truth.
- I let go of all judgment, perception, and conviction that dowsing with a pendulum to know the truth is challenging.
- I choose to let go of the need to believe that dowsing with a pendulum to know the truth is challenging.
- I release all judgment, perception, and conviction that I will receive wrong answers if I work with my higher self using a pendulum.

Any thoughts and beliefs that are actively released from your subconscious mind should always be replaced with a positive statement. This is why you should always recite replacing statements as well.

Step 3: Recite Replacing Statements

Reciting and replacing statements loudly with conviction, clear intention, and focus is vital in rewiring your brain. This makes working with a pendulum chart and your higher self significantly easier.

The following are some replacement statements that you can recite:

- I now command my subconscious mind to wholly believe and accept that I can receive accurate answers and helpful guidance from my superconscious mind and higher self by using a pendulum chart.
- I believe I am always optimistic when working with my superconscious mind and higher self when performing pendulum dowsing.
- I know exactly what it feels like to be working with my superconscious mind and higher self with conviction, belief, positivity, and trust.
- I fully comprehend how it feels to use pendulum charts and pendulum dowsing as an effective means of communication with my spirit guides and higher self. I do it with trust, conviction, and positivity.
- I find it effortless to use pendulums and pendulum charts to communicate with my superconscious mind and higher self to obtain beneficial answers to my questions.

Types of Pendulum Charts

Pendulum charts come in numerous shapes and forms. You can find printable templates online for diverse purposes. However, learning how to make your own charts allows you to personalize them and tailor them to your needs. Creating your own pendulum charts enables you to ask more specific questions and yield accurate answers.

In this section, you'll find step-by-step instructions on creating each type of pendulum chart, from the simple "Yes" or "No" charts to more complex ones. You'll come to understand when and how to use each of these charts.

"Yes" or "No" Pendulum Chart

You can use this chart to ask simple and direct questions that require yes/no answers. As mentioned previously, you should start your pendulum dowsing or divination session with these types of questions to ensure that you're actively communicating with your higher self.

How to Make the Pendulum Chart

Grab a standard-sized paper and a pen or pencil. Keep the paper in a portrait perspective (not landscape). In the middle of the paper, draw a small circle on the left side and another on the right using a protractor. Draw an oblong box at the bottom center and another at the top. Write the word "yes" in the circle on the left and the word "no" in the other circle. Write the word "maybe" in the oblong box at the bottom and the words "not at this time" in the other oblong.

How to Use the Pendulum Chart

Remind yourself of the intention of the ball of white golden light on top of you being connected to your higher self. With this intention in mind, follow these steps:

1. Use your consciousness to swing the pendulum from front to back. Say, "This means a "yes" answer."
2. Use your consciousness to swing the pendulum from left to right. Say, "This means a "no" answer."
3. Repeat both steps until you're confident that these answers have been established.
4. Ask the following questions:
    - "Higher self, am I a woman?"
    - "Higher self, am I a man?"

The pendulum should move towards either the "yes" or "no," depending on the correct answer. The pendulum should still give you a satisfactory answer if you identify as neither a man nor a woman.

Don't fret if it doesn't move in the right direction right away. Keep practicing several times until you get the correct answer. Always direct the question to your higher self and not to the pendulum or your ego self.

Half Shape Pendulum Chart

Half shape pendulum charts are typically used to ask relationship-related questions. However, you can use them to ask about a broad range of subjects.

How to Make the Pendulum Chart

Grab a standard-size sheet of paper and use it from a landscape perspective. Draw an upwards half-circle across the entire width and length of the paper. Draw a smaller half-circle within it, leaving enough space to write between both boundaries.

- **Relationship Pendulum Chart**

Divide the space between both half-circles into four equal sections. Write each of these words in an individual section: "physical," "spiritual," "mental," and "emotional."

Divide the area inside the small half-circle into three equal sections. Write each of these words in an individual section: "short," "medium," and "long."

- **Numbered Pendulum Chart**

Divide the half-circles into ten equal sections. Use the space between them to number each section from 10 to 100 percent in increments of ten (10%, 20%, 30%, 40%, etc.).

- **Multiple Choice Pendulum Chart**

Use this pendulum chart if you're stuck between several choices. You can divide it into as many sections as you like. Say you picked out five restaurant options, but you're struggling to choose one for your upcoming date. In that case, you'll split the chart into five sections, writing the name of one restaurant in each of the sections.

How to Use the Pendulum Chart

- **Relationship Pendulum Chart**

Ask the following questions:

1. What type of relationship is this?

The pendulum should swing along the four sections between both half-circles before it lands on an answer.

2. How long will we be together?

The pendulum should swing along the three sections in the smaller half-circle before it lands on an answer.

- **Numbered Pendulum Chart**

Ask questions that require numerical or percent-based answers. Start by asking: How accurate is this pendulum?

You may want to balance the pendulum depending on the answer you receive.

- **Multiple Choice Pendulum Chart**

Ask your questions and wait for the pendulum to land on the answers.

For example, if you're trying to decide on a restaurant, you can ask the following questions:

1. Which of these restaurants serves the best food?
2. Which of these restaurants has the best ambiance?
3. Which of these restaurants offers the best value for money?
4. Which of these restaurants has the highest hygienic standards?

Full Shape Pendulum Chart

Last but not least, this type of chart can be used to answer very specific questions in a wide range of subjects.

How to Make the Pendulum Chart

Use a protractor to draw a circle on a standard-size sheet of paper. Keeping the paper in a portrait perspective, make the circle as large as possible. Draw a smaller circle inside. Draw a line down the center of the circles, splitting them in half. Divide each of the circles into as many sections as you like. The sections on the upper left side of the circle are called "inside chart left," and the others are called "outside chart left." The sections in the upper right side of the circle are called "inside chart right," and the others are called "outside chart right."

How to Use the Pendulum Chart

When using this chart, begin by asking for general answers before moving on to more specific ones. Let's say you're still choosing between restaurants, only this time, you're choosing between four cuisines and 16 different restaurants (four restaurants for each cuisine).

In that case, you'll split the area between the boundaries of both circles into 4 equal sections. You can write the words "Italian," "Japanese," "Mediterranean," and "Chinese" (one in each section). You'll split the smaller circle into 16 equal sections and write the names of four Italian restaurants in the sections below the word "Italian," four Japanese restaurants in the sections below the word "Japanese," and so on.

Then, you'll ask the pendulum questions like:
1. Which of these cuisines has the healthiest food?
2. Which of these cuisines uses most of my favorite ingredients?

Once you settle on a cuisine, you can ask questions that will allow you to choose between the corresponding restaurants.

Congratulations! You now know everything you need to do to prepare yourself for this divination technique. You also know how to create and use various types of pendulum charts. This knowledge is bound to serve you as you keep developing your pendulum-wielding skills. Now, you're ready to move on to using the pendulum for spiritual healing.

Chapter 8: Pendulums for Spiritual Healing

This chapter explores the practice of spiritual energy healing using a pendulum in more depth. You'll understand how to use a pendulum as a diagnostic, cleansing, and healing tool. Upon reading this chapter, you'll learn how to scan the body and check the status of your chakras using the pendulum. You'll also find out how to incorporate this tool into Reiki practices and how to use it to balance your chakras.

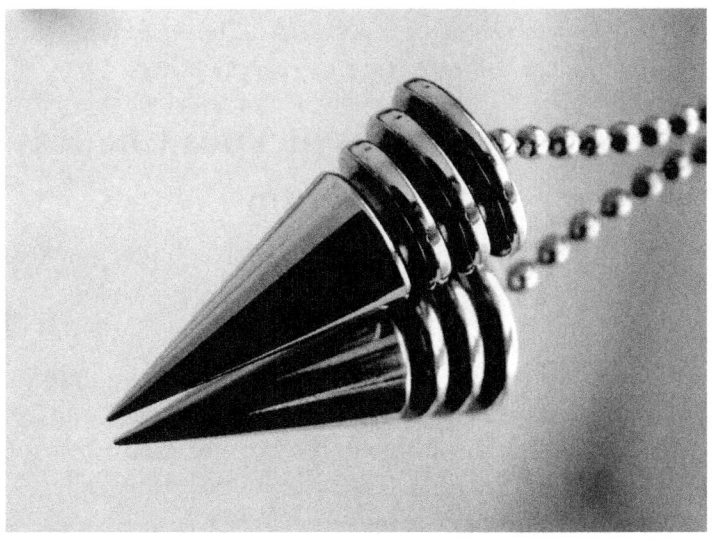

The energy flow generated by the chakras is amplified by the pendulum.
https://pixabay.com/es/photos/p%c3%a9ndulo-p%c3%a9ndulo-de-oro-reflexi%c3%b3n-686680/

Scanning the Body with a Pendulum

Pendulums are among the best tools to scan the body and determine the state of the chakras. This is because the pendulum amplifies the energy flow generated by the chakras. You can get a sense of the state of your chakras by observing the way that the pendulum swings – its movement is a manifestation of the energy produced by each chakra.

What Is the Chakra System?

The chakra system holds the "prana," or energy, in the body. The word "chakra" is Sanskrit for disk or wheel, which makes sense because, according to Ayurvedic medicine, the chakras are wheels of energy that can be found at several points along the body. While we have 114 chakras in total, the seven main chakras are located along the spine. They start at its base, extending all the way to the crown of the head.

Our behaviors, feelings, thoughts, experiences, and memories affect the chakras' energy. They directly impact our current and future physical, mental, social, and emotional health. We are at our healthiest when all our chakras are unblocked. This is because open chakras enable the free flow of energy throughout the body. When this occurs, our mind, body, and spirit exist in harmony.

Our chakras are constantly opening and closing, depending on our feelings, thoughts, and dynamics of life. These energy centers are constantly trying to align with the changing energy flows.

How to Check the Status of Your Chakras with a Pendulum

You can do several things to check on the state of your chakras using a pendulum. Here are some of the methods you can use:

Ask for Help

To use this method, you'll need a pendulum and the help of another person. The pendulum doesn't have to be programmed, but before you start, you must be clear about who will direct your questions. Both of you should start by meditating or practicing mindfulness techniques. You must have a clear mind and no expectations whatsoever.

To start off, you need to lie down on your back. Ask your helper to hold the pendulum just a few inches over your body. Have them hold it above each chakra for as long as they need to observe the pendulum's motion. They should write down the direction of the swinging of the chakra. When they've finished, turn over on your stomach and ask them to repeat the process.

Compare the first and second readings and watch out for any differences. Notice the force of the swing and its direction for each of the chakras. The greater the swing, the more energy is in that chakra. Ideally, you want all your chakras to be open and generate equally comparable swings. That said, chances are you'll find discrepancies between each chakra from both sets of readings.

Taking the time to determine these differences can help you identify the imbalances in your body and the problems you need to address. Here is a guide you can use to determine what each pendulum swing means:

- **Clockwise:** Open chakra, balanced, and free-flowing energy
- **Counterclockwise:** Closed chakra, out of balance, and restricted or blocked energy flow
- **A Straight Line in Either Direction:** Partially closed or open chakra, imbalance, and partial blockage of energy flow
- **Elliptical:** An imbalance in the right or left side of the chakra, which can be out of balance on either side while energy is still flowing
- **No Movement:** Blocked chakra, no flow of energy, or full blockage.

Use the Chakra Symbols as a Proxy

Suppose you don't wish to ask for someone's help. In that case, you can check your chakra's status using any pendulum and a colored printout that includes the symbol of each of the seven chakras. Declare who you're asking your questions to, whether they're your spirit guides, superconscious mind, or higher self. Clear your mind by performing breathing exercises or any mindfulness technique of your choice.

The colored printout will represent your own chakras. Rest the paper on a table and start only when you're in the right headspace. Hold the pendulum a few inches over each symbol. Visualize each area of your body during the whole process. For example, visualize your lower back or spine as you hold the pendulum over the root chakra symbol.

Many people accidentally visualize the answer to the pendulum – you should be careful not to do this. Write down your observations regarding the size and direction of the pendulum swing, and use the guide above to interpret your readings.

Use a Pendulum Chart

You can also print out a chakra pendulum chart to scan your body. The pendulum you use doesn't need to be programmed. If you don't have a printer, use the previous chapter as a guide on creating your own pendulum chart.

Create a half shape chart and divide it into seven equal half-circle sections. In the space between the boundaries of each half-circle, write the names of the chakras (each in a different section). You can color each section with the color of its corresponding chakra. If you can, draw each symbol or cut and paste tiny printouts of the symbols. In the smaller half-circle, you may write the name of each chakra in Sanskrit and the areas they affect. For example, in the root chakra section, you may write Muladhara and grounding, balance, stability, nourishment, strength, physical health, family, security, etc.

Clear your mind using a mindfulness technique (you may use the golden white light visualization technique from the previous chapter), and be clear about who you're directing your questions to. Place the chart on a desk and hold the pendulum over the center of the chart.

Ask your higher self or superconscious mind specific questions like:
1. Which of the chakras is open?
2. Which of the chakras holds the highest energy today?
3. Which of the chakras do I need to pay attention to the most?
4. Which of the chakras is contributing to my anxiety today?
5. Which of the chakras has a restricted flow of energy?

Your questions should be concise and straightforward enough to elicit a helpful answer from the pendulum. For example, you cannot ask vague questions like "What is the state of my chakras?"

Observe the swinging of the pendulum. If you ask it about your closed chakras, it will swing through the chakras that need the most attention, then stop or return to the root chakra it moved toward. If you ask which of your chakras are open and it swings clockwise, then all your chakras are open. By contrast, a counterclockwise movement indicates that all your chakras are closed.

Using a Pendulum in Reiki

If you wish to do reiki, relying on the pendulum is not advised throughout the entire healing session. Reiki healing is all about maintaining a connection with the person you're practicing with. Using a pendulum and paying attention to its movement throughout the entire session can prevent you from doing so.

Using a pendulum at the beginning of a reiki healing session allows you to identify the person's needs. It also helps you to determine if all the issues are addressed during the session. Pendulums are mainly used in reiki for two purposes: to determine each chakra's status and identify the crystals that should be used in the session.

What Is Reiki?

Reiki is a form of energy healing that can help induce tranquility and relaxation. This traditional Japanese technique aims to reduce anxiety and stress. Reiki practitioners rely on their hands and gentle touch to transmit energy to your body. This enhances the flow of energy and promotes balance, which encourages healing.

Reiki is a complementary, holistic healing technique focusing on emotional, mental, physical, and spiritual aspects. It can help bring the body to a meditative state and stimulate self-healing. This healing technique supports one's general well-being by strengthening the immune system, alleviating physical and emotional pain, relieving tension, and even promoting the healing of bones and tissues after serious injuries or surgery.

Individuals who undergo rigorous treatments like dialysis, surgery, radiation, and chemotherapy often turn to reiki for support. This medical and therapeutic treatment instills feelings of peace, security, wellness, and relaxation. That said, it's not considered an alternative medicine technique because it can't be a substitute for traditional treatments. It mainly accelerates the healing process and makes medical treatments more efficient.

Regular reiki sessions can keep you healthy if you don't struggle with particular ailments. They serve as good preventative medical techniques to help you deal with stress more efficiently.

Reiki practitioners act as a middleman between you and the main source of the prana, the ultimate universal life force. They use their hands to deliver this energy to your body. Your body is smart enough to accept only the amount of energy needed to thrive – it doesn't matter what the reiki master believes you need.

How to Use a Pendulum in a Reiki Healing Session

Even if you aren't a reiki master or practitioner, you can still practice this technique with a friend. Try to take it lightly, and don't forget to enjoy it, especially if you're new to this healing method. None of us maintain perfectly balanced chakras at all times, which is entirely normal.

Don't panic if the pendulum swings counterclockwise, indicating a blocked chakra. Freaking out will only cause your friend to worry even though they're fine. A blocked chakra indicates that your friend is experiencing a rough patch in life or is lacking some guidance and a sense of purpose. Fortunately, using a pendulum in reiki can help you determine the type of healing crystal your friend needs to promote a better flow of energy and restore balance to their chakra system.

Follow these practical steps if you wish to use a pendulum in a reiki session:

Step 1: Ask your friend to lie down on their back with their eyes closed. Tell them to draw in a couple of deep breaths and encourage them to clear their minds. If needed, you can walk them through guided meditation or breathing exercises. Have them call in their higher self. As a practitioner, you should also do the same – call in your healing or spirit guides and your higher self.

Step 2: Hold the pendulum a few inches over each of the seven chakras. Pause at each one for a moment to ask if this chakra is open. For example, you can ask, "Is (your friend's name) root chakra open?"

Step 3: As you ask each question, lightly swing the pendulum clockwise. Allow it to settle freely in any direction that it wants after you rotate it. In addition to the guide provided earlier in this chapter, you can use the direction of the swing to determine the degree of openness or closedness. For instance, if you get a 45-degree swing, this would indicate that the chakra is half open. An 80-degree swing, on the other hand, suggests that the chakra is mostly open. Use 90 degrees as your ceiling.

Follow these instructions to draw a chart that you can use for guidance:
1. Draw a vertical line down the center of the paper.
2. Draw a horizontal line halfway through the first line.
3. You should be left with what looks like the coordinate plane you used to draw in math class.
4. Draw a diagonal line that cuts through the middle of the first and third quadrants (upper right side to lower left side of the plane).
5. Draw another diagonal line that cuts through the middle of the second and fourth quadrants (upper left side to lower right side of the plane).
6. You should now have 8 equal sections.
   - The pendulum moving along the vertical line indicates a healthy or open chakra.
   - If the pendulum moves along the horizontal line, this indicates a closed or unhealthy chakra.
   - If the pendulum moves along the first diagonal line (upper right to lower left), this indicates a 50% open, overactive chakra.
   - If the pendulum moves along the second diagonal line (upper left to lower right), this indicates a 50% open, underactive chakra.

Now that you have a visual of the chart, memorize the directions and hold the pendulum directly over your friend's chakra. Only use the chart as a reference if you need it.

If you're a reiki practitioner, you should always ask your client if there's something they'd like to address during the healing session. Also, ask them if there's something you need to know about their current mental, emotional, spiritual, and physical state of health. Make sure to do that only after you use your intuition to determine the status of the chakras, as any upfront knowledge can lead to biased results. The energies in certain aspects of our lives manifest as imbalances in the chakras. For example, if a person struggles with relationships, they must work on their sacral and heart chakras.

After you've determined the status of the chakras, use the pendulum to determine which healing crystal to use.

What Are Healing Crystals?

When used correctly, healing crystals can deliver the powerful healing energy of the Earth. They generate positive and energizing vibrations that promote peace of mind and allow you to feel more energetic.

You can use numerous healing crystals, each of which uniquely affects the mind, body, and spirit. The vibrations emitted by each crystal are determined by how its molecules and atoms are arranged and how they interact and move.

Since our bodies are dynamic, complex, and electromagnetic, we always have spiritual, physical, mental, and emotional energy fields flowing through and around us. This means that crystals' energies and vibrations can affect us when they interact with our energy fields.

How to Use a Pendulum to Choose a Crystal to Work With

Using a pendulum to determine which healing crystal to work with is a very easy feat. Here is how you can do it:

Step 1: Arrange your healing crystals on a flat surface.

Step 2: Ask your higher self to guide you toward those it believes will benefit your friend (or client) the most.

Step 3: Gently hold the pendulum over your crystal collection and search for and observe its movement. Your intuition and indicators from the pendulum will help you to choose the right crystal.

Step 4: You must trust that your higher self and spirit guide will guide you toward the right crystal for this to work.

Balancing the Chakras with a Pendulum

Besides determining the status of your chakras, you can also use a pendulum to balance your chakra system. Here's how you can do it:

Cleansing Your Pendulum

You must cleanse your pendulum before you use it in any healing or balancing work. You also need to do this if you decide to work with crystals. This can help you get rid of any blockages and negative vibrations. It allows you to deliver the right message to your body effectively.

As you've seen, you can cleanse your pendulum or crystal via smudging. You can also run it underwater, allow it to recharge under the full moon or sunlight, or bury it in soil. If you plan to use sunlight to recharge your pendulum or crystal, make sure not to leave it there too long, as it may hinder its function.

In parallel, ensure you're ready before working with a pendulum. Take a couple of deep breaths and practice some visualization or grounding techniques. You can meditate for a while or retreat to a quiet spot. Do whatever it takes to put your thoughts on mute, disconnect from the external world, and get in touch with your deeper self. When you're ready, you can start balancing your chakras.

How to Balance the Chakras with a Pendulum

Hold the pendulum over each of your chakras in order. The pendulum will begin to show you the state of each of your chakras. Once that's done, go back to your root chakra and start moving along each of your chakras again. Use your intuition and the pendulum's swinging to determine how long you should stay above each energy center.

Make sure that your intention is clear – inviting all your chakras to fall into balance and harmony. Harmony, in essence, is the universe's natural frequency. You don't need to do anything except ask and allow your body to heal itself. Trust in its wisdom to do so.

If you're practicing on someone else, you must get them to trust in their body's ability to heal itself. You can do that by talking to them about what each chakra represents as you hold the pendulum over them. Explain their functions and how they work. That way, your friend or client will eventually let go of any mental blockages and believe in their self-healing powers.

Even though the pendulum is widely known as a diagnostic tool, you can simply use it to balance your chakras by asking your body to balance itself. Acknowledging your body's wisdom and power is enough to stimulate realignment. Once you believe you've addressed all these issues, return to the root chakra and start moving along the energy centers one last time. Make sure they're all open and that the pendulum is swinging in the same direction and with the same level of force for each of them. Don't worry if you don't receive the desired results right away. The more you practice working with pendulums and trusting your intuition, the easier and more enjoyable it will get.

Our bodies are more powerful than we could ever realize. We don't need to rely on other people and tools to feel balanced and at peace. Practicing reiki and working with pendulums stimulates and supports the natural self-healing abilities of the human body.

Chapter 9: Enhancing Your Pendulum Intuition

The world of divination is vast and versatile, involving various practices, including pendulum reading. While these practices may differ from one another, they share the same foundation. To truly practice the art of divination, you need to be in touch with your intuition. You must be aware of the energies surrounding you and how they affect everything around you. Being in touch with your intuition means listening to it and trusting it.

To truly practice the art of divination, you need to be in touch with your intuition.
https://pixabay.com/es/photos/p%c3%a9ndulo-mapa-navegaci%c3%b3n-br%c3%bajula-1934311/

Intuition is key when practicing divination. You can theoretically learn how to read and use the pendulum, but your readings will lack accuracy and flavor if you're not using your intuition. Intuition is what separates practitioners from each other – everyone is different, and so is their intuition. One practitioner's intuition may highlight certain elements in your readings, while others might pick on different aspects. You may also receive the same reading from different interpreters, but each of them will explain it in their own way. In other words, everyone's intuition is unique. This is why every reading has its own flavor and style.

By the end of this chapter, you'll have garnered plenty of useful insights to develop your intuition and enhance your magical or spiritual practice using the pendulum.

What Is Intuition?

Intuition is a widely known and accepted term. You must have heard about intuition if you're familiar with any spiritual practice. Many people know about intuition or are familiar with the general meaning, but not everyone knows exactly what intuition entails.

Simply put, intuition is the voice that emanates from your higher self. Your higher self is connected to your soul, which is in tune with the universe. This means that once you unlock your intuition, you'll learn how to pick up on the universe's waves and messages. You'll learn how to be in harmony with the universe and achieve your soul's purpose.

Listening to your intuition is a sacred and divine practice. Acting according to your intuition harmonizes you with the energy of the universe. Being in harmony with the universe will make you feel at home, which is one of the main reasons you should practice listening to your higher self's voice. Besides, unlocking your intuition should be a priority if you want to become a pendulum interpreter.

Intuition is like a muscle. The more you use and maintain it, the stronger it gets. Strong intuition allows for accurate readings and sharp gut instincts. This muscle is located in your third eye chakra, also known as the Anja.

The Anja is the center of your intuition. It is the sixth chakra and is located in the center of your forehead. Anja is known as the pineal gland. Scientifically, the pineal gland is a small part of your brain responsible for the intuitive messages you receive. Knowing where the center is, is important because once you do, it becomes easier to activate your intuition and tap into it.

Listening to Your Intuition

Now that you know what intuition is, it's time to know what it feels and sounds like. Your intuition is a voice that comes from within you. It feels calm, serene, and certain. It is common to confuse intuition with the sound of reason or the nagging voice of anxiety, but it is neither one of those things. When your intuition speaks to you, you'll feel like it has a sense of knowing. This voice will not nag you or make you feel like you should do something the way anxiety does. The more you trust and develop it, the better you'll become at differentiating it from other voices.

Now, you may wonder how to listen to it, especially if you haven't mindfully chosen to listen to your intuition before. It is normal not to be sure at first. Hopefully, this chapter will guide and introduce you to various methods to help you listen to your higher self's voice.

In the meantime, one of the simplest ways to receive guidance with intuition is to ask the universe. Set your intention on unlocking your intuition, which will enable you to put out energy into the universe. The universe will respond by giving you guidance. This guidance may take many forms, but you'll know it when you see it. It is also vital to know that acting on your intentions is another way of putting energy into the universe. Remember that whatever you put into the universe will come back to you. Setting your intentions is not enough – your actions need to mirror them, too.

Intuition and Pendulum Reading

By now, you know how to use the pendulum and are aware of different methods you can use to practice interpreting the pendulum. You know how the pendulum gives you an answer and how it swings.

You may ask yourself why you need to be in tune with your intuition if the pendulum is there to give you the necessary answers. That is a fair question. In reality, interpreting the pendulum without listening to your intuition may not always result in accurate readings or in readings that make sense.

Sometimes, the universe, energies, and the supernatural realm speak to us in a language we may not understand. Your intuition is your translator, guiding you in deciphering the message that you receive from a pendulum reading. You may receive a visual message or experience a certain feeling when interpreting your pendulum. These messages your intuition picks up on may not appear as clearly through your pendulum.

The more you use your pendulum, the more you'll become familiar with it. You will notice that your pendulum moves differently every time you use it. You may not understand the pendulum's movement if you're not in tune with your intuition. This means you won't be able to decipher its response. So, your intuition is the main tool that will help you retrieve and correctly interpret your pendulum's answers. You'll be able to distinguish weak pendulum motions from stronger ones. You'll be able to understand your pendulum's "yes," "no," and "maybe" without using a chart.

Remember that your intuition will set you apart from other pendulum users. This isn't to say that certain users are better than others. However, every practitioner has their own unique style. Pendulum interpreters add their own flavor to their readings when they allow their intuition to guide them. This is why reading with intuition is essential and does not solely depend on the pendulum's movements. Ultimately, the input that your intuition offers is valuable and essential.

Scientific Studies on Intuition

The world abounds with skeptics who believe intuition is just another new-age spiritual nonsense. That is fair because, at the end of the day, many people find it difficult to believe in the unseen. Fortunately, numerous studies have targeted intuition to determine whether it exists and to understand it scientifically.

According to Dr. Lou Cozolino, science gives a clear explanation of intuition and gut instincts. Cozolino explains that these intuitive messages are a product of channels and neurons that process information in the brain.

As neuroscientist Antonio Damasio explains, intuition is a product of evolution. He refers to intuition as "somatic markers," arguing that the more humans evolve, the more their brains grow somatic markers that help them understand subconscious emotions, read the environment around them, and make quick decisions. Damasio explains that intuition has helped humans survive, increased their chances of survival, and avoided perilous outcomes.

Dr. Daryl Bem, an American psychologist, conducted a study with 1000 participants. Bem designed different experiments to understand intuition and study its functions. He found that human beings can sense something before it occurs. He also stated that, although humans do not have the ability to predict the future, they can feel it before it manifests in the physical world.

Dr. Bem told Cornell News that he doesn't know how humans have developed these sensitive antennas capable of feeling events before they occur. He further explained that intuition helps humans make faster decisions and boosts their chances of making better choices that are in tune with what is best for them.

The assistant clinical professor of psychiatry at UCLA, Dr. Judith Orloff, theorized that intuition is part of the brain's hippocampus and is connected to the gut. She states that maintaining a healthy gut is essential for clearer, intuitive messages.

Dr. Orloff states that paying attention to literal gut feelings is vital. For example, if you feel off around a certain person, then you should take it as a warning sign. This sign is your intuition telling you that it may be best not to interact with that person or trust them. Orloff claims that trusting these feelings can help you avoid many problems and negative outcomes. Additionally, she works with women who wish to develop their intuition. These women view their intuition as their supernatural power that aids them in becoming better leaders and making better decisions.

How to Unlock and Maintain Your Intuition

There are numerous methods you can use to access and develop your intuition. Of course, these methods are spiritual and will significantly add to your life. Not only will they help you with your intuition, but they'll also support your spiritual awakening journey. Generally speaking, there is no specific method you should stick to. What matters is to feel comfortable with whichever method or methods you choose.

Meditation

Silencing the mind is essential when it comes to listening to your intuition. This will help you discern your higher self's voice from others. In that regard, meditation will sharpen your focus and help clear your mental environment. The clearer your mind is, the easier it will be to feel centered and listen to your intuition clearly.

Multiple meditation techniques are designed to help you connect with your third eye. That said, checking in with yourself before you pick a meditation practice is important. Read about each of them to determine which one you would like to try first. If you're unsure which one to start with, try all of them. Once you do, you'll be able to decide which ones you want to use.

Remember that when it comes to spiritual practices, you must practice the methods you are most comfortable with. Meditation shouldn't make you feel anxious or pressured in any way. That said, you need to be emotionally aware enough when you are meditating. Practice what serves you, and simply discard the rest.

Mantra Meditation

Mantra meditation revolves around repeating the same word or sentence. Your intention is essential with this type of meditation. You'll be setting all your focus and energy on this one mantra which will act according to your intention. So, before you meditate, be sure to set your intention clearly.

Think of what you'll learn from this type of meditation. The outcome should be related to enhancing your intuition, so set your intentions and meditate. Pick a mantra and stick to it - you can pick any one. Here are some mantras you can use or draw inspiration from you to create your own:

- I clearly hear my intuition
- My intuition speaks to me
- I am in tune with my intuition
- I believe in my ability to develop my intuition
- My intuition will guide me toward greater spiritual horizons

There are no strict rules regarding how long you should meditate. The important thing is to take deep breaths as you meditate and refocus when you experience brain chatter, also known as the "monkey brain." If this happens to you, gently guide your focus onto your mantra. Be kind to yourself when you do this. Frustration may inevitably interrupt your flow, so do your best to maintain your balance and stay grounded.

Visualization Meditation

This type of meditation relies on the power of visualization. To visualize an image in your brain is to clearly paint a picture of your goal. Try to live the image you are seeing in your head. Feel what it would be like to live according to your image. For instance, as you try to unlock your intuition, picture yourself acting according to your intuition. Feel the peace and calmness that come with listening to this voice. Picture yourself living in harmony with yourself and the universe. Envision yourself interpreting accurate readings thanks to your intuition.

Focus on this imagery as you meditate. Again, you can meditate as long as you see fit. However, you should know that as a beginner, or if you haven't meditated in a while, it's best to meditate for short periods at a time. Begin with five minutes, then ten minutes, until you find a duration that effectively brings you closer to your deeper self and connects you with your intuition.

Crystals

Crystals are formed by Mother Nature. While they may have different energies, they're all pure and positive in nature. Each crystal boasts various properties and radiates different energies. This is why specific crystals react with certain wavelengths, making them suitable for a wide range of magical or spiritual practices.

This means that certain crystals vibrate and resonate with your own intuition. In other words, certain kinds of crystals can help you unlock your intuition and be in tune with it. Since Mother Nature is so gracious, you can choose from plenty of crystals to enhance your intuitive powers. For a refresher, these include:

- Labradorite
- Amethyst
- Lapis lazuli
- Purple fluorite
- Azurite
- Kyanite
- Sodalite
- Lepidolite
- Lolite
- Citrine
- Turquoise
- Black Obsidian
- Black Tourmaline
- Clear Quartz

Crystals work through connection and reciprocated energy. When choosing a crystal to develop your intuition, make sure that you feel connected to it first before using it. This connection might manifest as an attraction to a certain type, or one or several crystals may stand out to you. Experiment with these and check in with your feelings and intuition. Ask the universe for guidance and observe yourself to see which crystal sparks a feeling within you.

Once you've picked a crystal, as we've mentioned before, you'll need to cleanse it. You can do so with sound, incense, or water. You know that certain crystals can be prone to degradation if exposed to water or moisture, so make sure you select an appropriate type. Next comes the charging phase, which you can do through sunlight or moonlight or by burying it in soil.

Now that your crystal is charged, you may use it. Hold your crystal between your palms and speak your intention into it. Tell the crystal what you wish to have. For instance, tell it that you want to hear your intuition clearly or need help unlocking your third eye. Thank your crystal for its gifts, and keep it around you. You can wear it as jewelry or keep it next to you when you're meditating.

Ultimately, your intuition plays a major role when interpreting the pendulum or practicing divination. If you want to become a pendulum interpreter, then you must work on your intuition. Accessing your intuition is neither difficult nor impossible. You have everything it takes to unlock this voice within you. Understand that this voice has always been a part of you. Every method or activity you'll perform will help you find this voice. These methods will help you learn how to listen to your intuition and how to differentiate it from other voices. They will sharpen your higher self's voice, providing you with clarity and confidence for your magical or spiritual practice.

Give yourself the grace and kindness you deserve as you learn about and develop your intuition. Do not succumb to feelings of frustration or demotivation when you don't achieve the desired results right away. Keep in mind that enhancing your intuition is an ongoing journey, so it's important to practice, be consistent, and allow yourself enough time until you reach your spiritual destination. Hopefully, the knowledge and tips included in this chapter will enable you to tap into your full intuitive potential, which you'll employ to strengthen your pendulum practice.

Chapter 10: Pendulum Magic

The pendulum is one of the easiest divination tools you can use. Once you have learned its language and how to use it, everything becomes much easier in your journey. What's great is that there are no limits to what you can do with your pendulum - you can inquire about virtually anything you wish to know about.

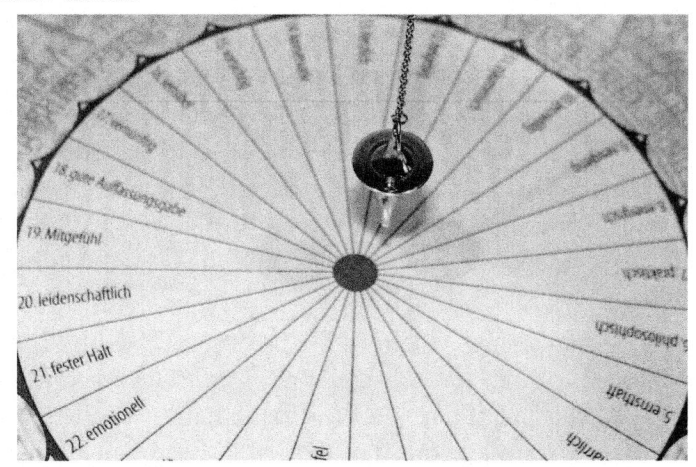

The pendulum is one of the easiest divination tools you can use.
https://pixabay.com/es/photos/p%c3%a9ndulo-paneles-de-p%c3%a9ndulo-tablero-242746/

As you know by now, there is magic in everything and everywhere around us. Pendulum magic is no different. You can use it with different divination tools and seek answers that you'll only find through the pendulum. This final chapter explores various methods and exercises you can engage in using the power of your pendulum.

Psychic Protection

It's always wise to protect yourself spiritually, regardless of whether or not you are a practitioner of the mystical. Think about it - you are mind, body, and soul. People spend time protecting their bodies from harm and do the same with their mental health, so why should it be any different for the soul?

Protecting yourself from psychic attacks is essential. If you're left unprotected, people can knowingly or unknowingly hurt you. If you believe in energies and how they work, you know that everyone is affected by the energies surrounding them. This means that a person can subconsciously send negative vibrations your way. Someone else may know exactly what they are doing and harm your energy on purpose.

Spiritualists always warn people about "psychic vampires." This term applies to those who feel rejuvenated after sucking the energy out of another person. Hopefully, you've never encountered a psychic vampire. Still, if you ever do, you must be prepared to ward off their negativity.

The Symptoms

To know whether you are being psychically attacked, you need to recognize what to look for. There are various ways in which an attack can show up, depending on who or what is attacking you. For instance, people who spend time around energy vampires usually feel significantly drained afterward. This pattern repeats itself until the person can connect the dots and understand what is happening to them. Other symptoms include low self-esteem and feeling unseen, unheard, and unworthy. While you may not feel all these symptoms at once, you'll feel like you have been energetically drained.

Other attacks may make you feel like you're always tired, constantly demotivated, and feeling low in general. These feelings will also be accompanied by daily nightmares, odd dreams, and experiencing bizarre circumstances. For example, you may suddenly feel the negative energy in the air or frequently find yourself in inextricable situations.

Protection
The Pendulum

Luckily, there are multiple ways to shield yourself from low-frequency energies. You can use the pendulum to identify the source of the attack. If there are people you are suspicious of, then write their names down on a dedicated chart and ask the pendulum to show you who is wishing harm upon you. You can also ask if this person is jealous of you, resents you, etc. After this part, you can proceed by asking the pendulum whether you should steer clear of certain people in your life.

Guard Your Aura

Shielding your aura is one of the best ways to protect your energy. Start by taking deep breaths, pausing, and then slowly exhaling. As you breathe in and out, imagine your aura growing in size. After that, take yourself out on a walk, or engage in an activity that benefits your aura. These can include laughing exercises, reading, working out, or getting a massage. Do whatever you feel the day calls for, as long as it strengthens your aura.

Crystals and Light Circles

According to psychics and energy healers, the bottom four chakras are most affected when people are energetically attacked. You can protect these areas by wearing crystals. Now, before you do, make sure to cleanse and charge them properly, then set your intentions.

Suppose you feel an attack and don't have your crystals on you. In that case, you can visualize a circle of light shielding you from unwanted energies. As you do so, guard your stomach and legs by covering them. You can cross your arms and legs or put a pillow on your stomach. These are easy ways to shield yourself until you wear your crystals or remove yourself from the situation altogether.

Spirit Guide Communication

According to spiritualists, every person was assigned a spirit team before birth. It is said that before your arrival on Earth, you were a soul in the spirit realm. You agreed to or chose to go back to earth in that realm. Before your spirit entered into your ego, it agreed to a contract with other spirits. In this pact, you and your spirit guides agreed to take this journey together. You were sent to Earth to accomplish your spirit's mission, and your spirit team will look after you.

Your spirit team loves you unconditionally and is always looking out for you. They are there for you in times of need, sending love, support, and blessings your way. Since your spirit team wants the best for you, getting their views and opinions will be interesting and enriching.

We often wish there was someone to guide us and help us find the right answers in life. If you've felt this way before, you don't need to keep wishing and wondering. You can simply ask your spirit guides.

You can communicate with your spirit guides in numerous ways. This section will explore communicating with your spirit team using the pendulum. This may sound daunting, but it really isn't. Once you talk to them, you'll feel at ease and at home. Here's what you need to get started.

First, find a comfortable spot in your home. It could be your meditation spot or next to your altar. Next, create a board and write down the following words: "yes," "no," and "maybe." If you don't want to create one, you can easily find one online. Remember that communicating with your spirit team is a deeply personal matter, so your board can have whatever you like on it. It could have other words and doesn't have to contain the standard answers. You can personalize this as much as you want.

With your board ready, you can finally grab your pendulum and connect with your spirit guides. You can get to know them, ask them questions, or talk to them about life and heed their advice.

After you've finished talking to your guides, thank them for your conversation. Keeping up communication with your team is always a good idea. Maintaining a relationship with your spirit team, who love and care for you, can be very soul-rewarding.

Past-Life Reading

If you believe in reincarnation, you know that every soul has experienced different lives over the course of its existence. Naturally, at some point in time, you must have felt curious about your past life. Who were you? Were you a woman or a man? What are your karmic debts? During which era did you live? Is there anyone in your life right now who was also with you in your past life? Did you have karmic relationships in this past life?

Some people would rather not know about their past life, but others do. Ultimately, it all comes down to your intuition. Your higher self will tell you whether it's a good idea to know about your previous life. If you feel the need to know about your past life, or your intuition is guiding you to get in touch with it, then this is a sign that you should explore this part of your soul's journey.

You can use your pendulum to delve back into your past life. Before you begin, you need to have patience, as this is a slow process. To start, write down your questions. Here are a few ideas:

- Was I a woman or a man in my most recent past life?
- Did I have a joyous life?
- Was I a good person?
- Did I fulfill my soul's purpose in my past life?
- Do I know anyone now from my past life?
- Do I have karmic relationships in this current life?
- How many times have I been reincarnated?

When asking the pendulum about your date of birth, be as specific as possible. For example, ask if you were born in the 18th, 19th, or 20th century. You can ask about each decade to know more. You can do the same with countries or continents, in which case you should get a map and see where your pendulum takes you. There is an infinity of things you can ask the pendulum about. Brainstorm and ask any question that stimulates your curiosity and that you feel brings you closer to your deeper spiritual self.

Numerous practitioners are concerned about their karmic debts, so they try to get as much information about it from their reading. Karmic debts are actions that you took in a past life. These actions may have caused an imbalance in your karma, meaning you'll have to make amends for it in your next life. If you feel preoccupied with your karmic debt, you might want to ask your pendulum about it.

Readers also ask about their karmic relationships. Karmic relationships involve people who knew each other in a past life. During their time together in their past life, they experienced obstacles that stood in the way of their growth. As a result, they meet again in their next life to make amends and grow together in their relationship.

Here are some questions you can ask your pendulum: Do I have karmic debts? What are they? Can I repay them in this life? How can I repay them? Do I have karmic relations in this life? Why? Who do I have a karmic relationship with?

Remember that the pendulum will move differently if you're not using a board, picture, or map. If you're not using any tools, the pendulum will move clockwise for "yes" and anticlockwise for "no."

Numerology

Do you often encounter a pattern of the same number? Have you ever wondered whether it was a coded message for you? Did you wonder why you keep seeing them? If your answer to these questions is "yes," you might be interested in numerology. This ancient divination practice was founded in China, then later popularized in Europe by Pythagoras. The idea behind numerology is that every number has a message of significance behind it. It teaches us that everything around us can be translated into numbers and that these numbers can help unveil coded messages.

Pendulum and Numerology

Many pendulum users combine numerology with pendulum magic. You can use these together to gather insights about the future or better understand synchronicities. While there are various ways to integrate these two practices, you first need to understand the meaning behind each number. The following chart details what each number signifies in numerology:

Number	General meanings
01	<ul><li>The self</li><li>Self-expression</li><li>Independence</li><li>Innovative</li></ul>
02	<ul><li>Duality</li><li>Equilibrium</li><li>Justice</li><li>Intuition</li><li>Supportive</li><li>Protective</li><li>Inclusive</li><li>Empathetic</li></ul>

| 03 | - Left-brain faculties
- Communication
- Artistic
- Optimism
- Jovial |
|---|---|
| 04 | - Proactive
- Patience
- Loyalty
- Restrictions
- Dependable
- Conscientious |
| 05 | - Love
- Freedom of expression
- Energetic
- Adventurous
- Creativity |
| 06 | - Healing
- Nurturing
- Left and right brain
- Anxiety
- Depression |
| 07 | - Analytical
- Spiritual
- Intellectual
- Philosophical |
| 08 | - Materialistic
- Accomplished
- Wisdom |

09	• Humanitarian • Sacrifice • Idealism • Responsible

According to occultist Richard Webster, the best way to gather insights about the future with pendulum numerology is to understand what each number represents and decipher its meaning according to the question asked. In other words, you may need to interpret these numbers differently according to your question.

To predict your future using numerology, Webster advises you to get 9 envelopes along with 9 cards. Label the cards from 1 to 9, and assign one card to each envelope. Now, scramble the envelopes until you forget the cards' placements.

As you shuffle the cards, think about your question. Try to be precise with your question - the more detailed, the better. If your question is too broad, then you may get a vague answer.

Place the 9 envelopes in a row and grab your pendulum. Ask your question and watch the pendulum work its magic. Gently hover the pendulum over the envelopes without moving it. Go over each card and observe the pendulum's movements. The pendulum should swing more vividly around a certain envelope, indicating that you have your answer. Now, open your envelope and see which number you have.

Here, you'll find an interpretation for each number to help you figure out an answer to your question.

New beginnings. It's time to be ambitious and show initiative toward your goals. Be patient. This is not the time to push your luck. Sit back, and what you have worked for will reward you. (1)

Be patient. This is not the time to push your luck. Sit back, and what you have worked for will reward you. (2)

Balance is key. It is important to prioritize your personal needs. Set time for work, and set some for playtime and relaxation. (3)

Slow progress. You might be feeling frustrated that your labor hasn't borne any fruit. Remember that growth takes time and that good things come to those who wait. (4)

Transformation. Brace yourself as you are about to experience some kind of change in your life. (5)

It is time to give back. The universe is inviting you to share your love and care with your family and loved ones. (6)

Feed your spirit. Now is the time to meditate, practice grounding, spend time with nature, and nurture your soul. (7)

Material gains. You may have been worrying about your finances lately. There's no need to be anxious. Maintain the balance between work and relaxation, and money will soon come your way. (8)

Replenishing. Now is the time to get rid of what doesn't serve you. Bid farewell to those who aren't good for you and relinquish any habits that don't serve your spiritual growth. (9)

Everyday Magic

As you can see, you can learn many special things from your pendulum. It can give you the kind of answers that would otherwise be impossible to find anywhere else. That said, there are other uses for your cherished tool. Since magic exists everywhere and in everything, you can use your pendulum to learn about things in your everyday life, like retrieving lost objects, checking on your health, and interpreting dreams.

Finding Lost Items

Misplacing an item can be terribly frustrating, especially when you're in a hurry. Luckily, you don't have to spend time scavenging for it or succumb to anxiety. You can simply just ask your pendulum, and it will answer you.

Grab your pendulum and visualize the item you're looking for. Ask the pendulum if your item is located around your house, in your car, at the office, etc. Keep asking your pendulum and wait for an answer. The best way to start is with broad questions, then move on to detailed ones. You can also ask if someone stole it or has "borrowed" it without your knowledge.

You can also do the same with people or pets. For this, get a picture of the person or animal in question. You can also grab a map or a piece of paper with different locations and start asking the pendulum. Many pendulum users do this to help themselves or others when they've lost someone they love. This method can yield effective and fast results if done correctly and with the right intention.

Inquiring about Your Health

It's normal for everyone to worry about their health from time to time. However, when one thinks of their health, their mind goes directly to their physical state. Are they consuming healthy food? Should they follow a new workout routine? Are they taking their medications? While all of these questions are valid, keeping a healthy body is not synonymous with physical well-being.

Your health is composed of mainly four factors: physical, mental, emotional, and spiritual health. Each must be addressed and taken care of properly. Unfortunately, in our modern, fast-paced lives, one can often lose sight of their well-being.

While neglecting your emotional and spiritual health won't kill you, it will certainly make your life challenging. Taking the time to nurture your soul and care for yourself emotionally and mentally will be rewarding beyond imagination.

If you're unsure about your health status, you can ask your pendulum. You can ask which of the four factors requires the most attention. Which parts need nourishment and extra care? The answer may surprise you. Once you can get straight answers to simple questions, you can ask your pendulum for ways to take care of your soul. How can you bolster your emotional health? What is the best way to heal yourself mentally? You can set a day where you take care of your needs. Again, seeking answers from your pendulum should never be a substitute for a medical check-up with a health professional.

In parallel to your pendulum practice, you can learn more about your mental health with self-help books or by going to therapy. You can get a massage once a month. You can meditate and practice breathing exercises to feed your spirit. You can also attune to your emotions and feelings by journaling and spending some of your time in nature.

Dreams

Many people focus on their dream work for a variety of reasons. Most believe that the subconscious speaks to them through their dreams. Others believe that dreams transport them to a different realm or an alternative life. Some even like to write down their dreams to practice lucid dreaming and astral projection. If you're as interested in your dreams as these people are, you may want to start paying more attention to them.

If you haven't done this before, then you may wake up forgetting your dreams or remembering them by chance. To keep track of your dreams, you should start journaling. This will help you remember your dreams more vividly. However, this method isn't completely error-proof. If you wake up one day and forget your dreams, you can always ask your pendulum about them.

Before you ask your pendulum, try to remember how your dream felt. This will help you narrow down your questions. You can then start with broad questions: was it a good dream or a bad one? What were you doing in the dream? Here, you can list down different activities (watching TV, cooking, working out, or even flying). Was there anyone with you in the dream? Did it have a coded spiritual message? What should you learn from this dream?

After you've finished with your questions, journal about your experience with the pendulum. Write down your questions and describe the pendulum's movements. This will help you progress and hone your craft when it comes to using your pendulum.

All in all, pendulum magic is exceptionally useful and versatile. It's one of the rare tools you can easily integrate with other divination practices to give you answers to anything you inquire about.

As you've seen, you can use your pendulum to protect yourself energetically. You can ask if you are being energetically attacked and which tools you need to protect yourself spiritually. You can also communicate with your spirit guides using the pendulum. You'll see how easily the conversation flows between you, especially when you're around such loving and nurturing spirits.

The pendulum can also help paint a picture of your past life. All you need to do is narrow down your questions and write down their answers. You do not have to complete a past life reading in one sit down. This can be done over a few days if you like. Incorporating numerology into your pendulum reading could give you a richer insight. Pendulum magic is a vast world; there are numerous magical rituals that you can try for yourself. Some activities are mentioned here, but you can also branch out by practicing other ones. Finally, you can practice magic daily by asking about lost items, health, and dreams.

Conclusion

Despite the plethora of divination tools being used today, pendulums are and continue to be the most popular ones throughout history. This is due to their straightforward usage and easy techniques. Divination practices open up your mind to a vast, unexplored world. Once you open yourself up to this soulful practice, you'll be able to explore your psychic powers to understand different aspects and viewpoints of life. You'll see the world with a new pair of eyes once you master the art of pendulum magic. An older version of you would be surprised at the decisions you may make once you start allowing your intuition to guide you toward success.

Using your pendulum to explore different paths in your life will certainly prove helpful. This way, you can attune yourself to your intuition and get nudged toward the right answers in life. While it is sometimes challenging to trust your intuition, opening yourself up to this new level of wisdom might be just what will guide you in the right direction. Once you connect with your pendulum, know for certain that it will be a lifelong friend to you. Even years after they've worn out and broken down, they will be a memory of all the good decisions you made.

When using the pendulum, you must show trust, patience, and perseverance to obtain successful results. And while you might not always get the correct predictions or outcomes you expected, losing hope in this practice is not the way forward. So, move slowly and lovingly in this practice. Soon enough, you'll become a master of pendulum magic, taking readings for your friends and loved ones. Make sure you practice it regularly, and do not be tempted to give up if it's not working. Perhaps you just need a change of mind, a change of scenery, or a change of heart to get better results.

It's also important that you don't compare your pendulum journey with those of others. This is something everyone will experience in their own unique way. Know that there is no right or wrong way to use the pendulum. Simply remember what you've learned from this book and other resources, and you'll master different pendulum techniques in no time. Get your pendulums out and create a magical connection between your pendulums and your self-intuition.

Make sure you select a pendulum that has sparked something in you. Embrace this divination tool as something you love and care for; soon enough, you'll feel a bond so strong that it will be unbreakable. This connection may or may not change your entire life, but it will give you genuinely good advice whenever you need it. Take all the help you can get from this book, apply all your knowledge to practical techniques, and witness real change in your life. Always remember that the results obtained from these techniques aren't set in stone and that the final decision will always depend on you. Good luck!

Part 2: Divination for Beginners

Unlocking Future Prediction Methods of Astrology, Tarot, Numerology, Palm Reading, Crystals, Runes, and Crystal Ball Reading

Introduction

Divination is an age-old method used to gain insight into situations, events, and connections made in the future. No divination method will tell you the exact future. The answers revealed are all subject to interpretation. And there are different techniques designed to gather knowledge about future happenings, but they can only serve as an inspiration. Interpreting the future means looking into something that is constantly changing. No event is fixed - and this is mainly due to free will.

You can ask for a specific answer, but how you interpret it and how it will come to reality are two different things. Your thoughts and actions at the time of reading will influence how you map out your future and whether the results you predict come true. No matter how clearly you see the picture of your future, the outcome can change as soon as you change any aspect of your behavior. And you're free to change your mind anytime you want to.

Since the beginning of time, there have been examples of divination in many different cultures. Some of these practices started as simple observations of events happening on Earth. Other cultures went beyond observing, fashioning tools with the specific intent of discerning what the future holds for them. In either case, the energy of the diviner carries the primary influence alongside the universal energy of life. When divination is done for another person, their energy will mix these forces and provide answers in one form or another.

Another crucial aspect of divination is the question you'll be asking. The type of answers you're interested in will also influence which divinatory method is the best to answer your specific question. You may feel that a particular technique provides you with better insight into critical questions about your life's potential. Some also find it easier to collect energy by using specific tools, which facilitate the revelation of the answers they are looking for. The questions and their answers also need to reflect your situation. Although suitable for beginners, "yes" or "no" questions won't reveal much about the future. They can only confirm something but not how it comes to be. When asking more open-ended questions, you'll be more likely to access the pool of available information about any area of life you want to know about.

This thorough and practical guide provides all the tools you need to discover your future. It is a perfect stepping stone for those wanting to delve into divinatory practices like astrology, tarot, numerology, chiromancy, palmistry, and runic divination. Just as these art forms gave answers to ancient civilizations, they will provide you with information about the past, present, and future in the same way. Whether you're just looking to find the perfect technique or are a skilled practitioner seeking to reconnect with a specific divinatory form, you'll find the way to do so throughout this book.

Whichever method you choose to add to your practices, the key to mastering it will be working on your intuition. After all, the answers you receive can only be interpreted correctly if you recognize whether they align with your values. In most cases, this is the first meaning that comes to mind, as this is the closest one to your true self. If you're ready to explore which divinatory art resonates with your values and personality, read on, and you'll find out.

Chapter 1: Divination Now and Then

Divination is one of the most interesting yet little-known magical practices today. When people think of divination, they generally think of Harry Potter, Professor Trewlaney, crystal balls, and reading tea leaves. While Harry Potter has undoubtedly brought the practice of divination to widespread notice, there's far more to this practice than is to be found in the books and movies.

Divination is widespread and found worldwide.
https://www.pexels.com/photo/woman-in-red-hat-and-black-outfit-sitting-on-the-bed-while-holding-a-crystal-ball-6806745/

Divination is essentially an attempt to improve our insight into questions and situations that don't have a clear solution. Today, it is generally considered an attempt to foretell the future. However, there's more to divination than simply reading and predicting the future.

This book details and helps you understand divination, as well as introduces you to how it is best practiced. However, before you can do that, understanding its history will give you a solid base of knowledge to work from.

History of Divination

Divination was known to have been practiced as far back as the ancient Greeks and Romans. In ancient Greece, oracles were held in high respect and were considered to be a link between the gods and humans. In fact, the divinatory revelations of the oracles were considered to have literally been words from the gods.

Indeed, oracles were in high demand. However, their divinatory revelations were so rare that getting a prediction from an oracle became a valued commodity in ancient Greece.

Oracles were not the only vessels of divination in ancient Greece, nor were they the most common. Seers filled this role.

Unlike oracles, seers did not speak the words of the gods directly, and contrary to their name, they did not "see" the future. Rather, they read and interpreted signs offered by the gods using methods such as reading the entrails of animals that had been ritually sacrificed and reading the signs of the birds. Seers, unlike oracles, could only answer yes or no questions.

Seers were so essential to life in ancient Greece and Rome that they were often found on battlegrounds and in army camps, as generals would need to consult with them on battlefield tactics. Without the seer's approval (through the reading of certain signs), battles would not occur.

It should be noted that seers and oracles were not just common among the Greeks and Romans. They were also popular among the ancient Egyptians. One of the best-known mentions of an oracle and divination in antiquity is Alexander the Great's meeting with the Oracle of Amun at the Siwa Oasis.

While belief in divination dates back to antiquity, so does skepticism of the practice. Given the influence and power the seers and oracles held, many people were skeptical about the veracity of their claims. However, more people actually believed in their abilities. But, as years passed, there was a growing distrust in oracles which led to a decline in their popularity and use by the 1st century AD. Various forms of divination were practiced throughout the world, including astrology in India and the Middle and Near East and in Kabbalah by the Jews. In China, the I Ching (also known as the Yi Jing) is one of the oldest known divinatory texts and explores cleromancy, a form of divination also known as I Ching divination. This complex form of divination involves the use of yarrow stalks.

Divination can be practiced using instruments, as in I Ching divination, or through bodies, such as the divination of the Greek oracles. The practice is widespread and found worldwide.

Divination in the Middle Ages

While divination is carried out throughout the world, the prohibition of the craft found in some books of the Bible, combined with the growing popularity of Christianity, led to a decline in public popularity. People practicing forms of divination were often prosecuted and even put to death. One example is the Electorate of Saxony, whose laws from 1572 to 1661 say that it is against the law to tell the future, and the penalty is death.

At the same time, folk practitioners kept traditional versions of divination alive. While they were often punishable by death, they were just as often practiced. They were especially popular with people in the lower social classes.

Nonetheless, divination continued to be practiced in non-European countries. For example, Islamic countries promoted the study of astrology at a state level. Additionally, geomancy (divination with sand, rocks, or soil) was popular with people of all social classes and was used to divine prophecies.

Different forms of divination that were popular in Islamic countries included oneiromancy, or divination through dream interpretation, and the uniquely Islamic "science of letters," which involved the study of the Koran combined with mathematics.

In other parts of the world, Islamic divination involved the intervention of religious leaders, healers, and dedicated diviners. It also involved items like amulets. In fact, in West Africa, Islamic diviners were crucial to helping spread Islam around the continent.

The practice of divination also continued in Mesoamerica, with divinatory practices including scrying through mirrors, casting lots, and using kernels of maize to divine answers.

Divination Today

Today has seen a re-awakening of interest in the Western world. It is practiced as part of a variety of esoteric religious practices, including:

- Wicca
- Paganism
- Witchcraft
- Voodoo
- Santeria

Each religion has its own tools. Some, like Wicca, paganism, and witchcraft, use many different items as their divinatory tools.

In parts of India and Nepal, oracles who channel the gods in their bodies can still be found.

In Japan, divination involves traditional and foreign forms of divination, like Onmyōdō, I Ching divination, and tarot reading. The Chinese zodiac signs, cardinal directions, four elements, yin-yang, and planets all play key roles in modern Japanese divination. Tarot cards are so popular that there are multiple decks designed with Japanese culture in mind.

In Taiwan, Poe, or mood board divination (using two wooden blocks shaped like crescent moons), continues to be used. At the same time, the followers of the Serer religion in Senegal believe in hereditary rain priests who are believed to be able to divine the future.

Aside from "religious" divination, fortune-telling apps, websites, and individuals will offer to tell a person's fortune as a form of entertainment at carnivals and fairs. Today, the future is available to everyone who seeks it. However, these "gimmick divinations" are far less reliable and more generic than the answers offered through regular divinatory practice.

The desire to learn more about things to come is part of human nature, and as long as this desire remains a driving force behind our actions, divination will continue to play an important role worldwide.

How Divination Works

When people think of divination, they think of predictions of the future. Specifically, they think of it as forecasting and telling the future.

However, this is not the only thing that divination can do. Depending on the type of tradition of divination, it can also be diagnostic, a way to find answers to questions, advice, and guidelines to follow, as well as interventionist - that is, a way to intervene in an undesired potential future.

This is part of the reason divination is so popular. Not only does it tell the future, but some traditions also allow people to use this knowledge to change the future.

Keep in mind that this is not always possible. For example, Greek mythology is full of references to stories of people who heard unfortunate prophecies from the oracles and tried to subvert the future, such as Perseus's grandfather and Oedipus's father, only to end up being the cause of the prophecy coming true.

However, in many traditions, divination is seen as more of an insight into potential or a future that may potentially come true unless acted upon. This allows the person whose future is "being read" to determine whether it is something they wish to act on or not. Destiny is not an immutable law but can be changed depending on a person's actions, and divination gives a person a chance to be the author of those changes.

It should also be noted that divination is a living and constantly changing practice. People choose to interpret symbols differently, and existing symbols gain new meanings over time. Because divination often involves interpretation, reading for one person, and answering the same question, it may differ from one diviner to the next. This isn't to say that either is wrong - only that each provides a different perspective to the answer.

Types of Divination

As discussed, there are numerous divination traditions followed around the world. Many forms that fell out of favor due to religious persecution and witch hunts have, in the past 100 years or so, been gaining popularity again.

Given that there are hundreds of types of divination, listing them all is impossible. However, here are some of the most common forms of those practiced today and those which were more evident in the past:

Tarot Cards

Reading Tarot cards (also known as tarotmancy) involves much interpretation. While it seems like Tarot readers are "reading the future," they simply provide an interpretation of the most probable outcome defined by the cards. Tarot cards do not provide perfect insights into a person's future. In most cases, your future, as defined by the cards, is perpetually in flux and changeable.

Tarot is best regarded as a divinatory tool for self-improvement and reflection, providing you with a guide you can use to alter your life if need be.

Celtic Ogham

Also known as Ogham casting, this is a form of cleromancy. It involves using the Celtic Ogham alphabet carved on staves (or short sticks), casting them, then interpreting the patterns formed by how the staves fall.

Norse Runes

Also known as rune casting involves carving the Norse runes onto rocks, pebbles, or, traditionally, wood (one rune to a chosen material) and then casting them on a white linen sheet. Depending on how the runes land, divinatory interpretations are made.

Tasseomancy

Tasseomancy involves reading tea leaves or coffee grounds, though the former is more common. Tasseomancy is a good example of the living nature of divinatory. This is a relatively new divinatory practice that started in the 17th century.

You cannot do a tea reading without first having the leaves to read. Brew up a cup of tea with loose leaves; *do not remove* the leaves from the cup. Instead, let them settle at the bottom of the cup and then drink the tea until only the leaves are left. When only the wet leaves are left, give them a swirl until you see patterns emerge – this is when you can start to read.

Pallomancy

Pallomancy is one of the easiest forms of divination and involves using a pendulum. You can usually only ask yes or no questions for this form of divination, but it is a good introduction to the world of divinatory practices.

Pendulums are often used in conjunction with pendulum boards, tarot cards, and other magical tools. Some people even use a pendulum as a kind of dowsing rod.

Astrology

Also known as astromancy, this form of divination involves reading the movements and position of the planets, stars, and other celestial bodies. One of the most popular forms of astrology is drawing up and reading a person's birth chart, which is a comprehensive chart showing how each relevant celestial body was positioned in the night sky at the time of a person's birth.

There are different forms of astrology readings, depending on the purpose of the person's question. For example, some forms include horoscopic and natal astrology, electional astrology, sun sign astrology, and locational astrology. There are also different astrological traditions worldwide, including Indian astrology, Hellenistic astrology, Chinese astrology, and Western astrology.

Numerology

Numerology is a divinatory practice where those using it believe numbers hold enormous significance. Numerology involves studying the mystical relationships between numbers and how numbers affect events. Some numerical combinations are considered more potent and can be applied to different situations. For example, they may act as a reference to how a person should change their name.

Various numeric systems are used in numerological divination, including Pythagorean, Chaldean, Agrippan, and Kabbalistic. It can also be combined with astrology for a more informed insight into questions.

Palmistry

Also known as palm reading, this practice is about finding answers by studying a person's palm. There are many variations of this worldwide practice, which is popular in:

India and the Indian sub-continent

Persia

Sumeria

Greece

The Catholic Church banned the practice, and there were two papal edicts against it enforced by Popes Paul IV & Sixtus V.

This technique involves reading the lines on a person's palm and using them to make predictions. While palmistry has declined in popularity in the West, it remains enormously popular in other parts of the world, particularly in South and South-East Asian countries.

Crystal Divination

As its name suggests, Crystal divination uses crystals to make divinatory predictions. One of the most popular forms of crystal divination is crystal scrying or crystal ball reading, which involves looking at a crystal ball to see visions of the future.

Other types of crystal divination include crystal throwing. This is done by filling a pouch with stones, crystals, and gemstones and throwing them onto a premade grid. Predictions are made depending on where each stone falls on this grid.

You can either make your own personalized grid at home or find a pattern online.

Osteomancy

Osteomancy is about finding answers in the bones of animals or humans. The traditions of osteomancy differ around the world, and the bones are prepared in different ways, including:

Ceremonially burning them

Marking them with magical symbols

Mixing them in a pouch with other items

In the past, animals were often sacrificed specifically to use their bones for osteomancy. This rarely happens today, and it is common to use animal bones from animals that have died from natural causes or accidents.

Geomancy

Stones and socks can show patterns when they are cast together. You'll find patterns when casting smaller materials like soil and sand. These patterns can be read by those who know what to look for. It was common around Europe and Africa and was also particularly popular in Islamic countries.

Hydromancy

Where geomancy uses sand and soil for divination, hydromancy uses water for the same purposes. Some elements interpreted in a search for answers include the following elements:

Color.

Ripples.

The ebb and flow of disturbed water.

Lithomancy

Lithomancy involves using stones to tell the future. This form of divination has been around for thousands of years and can be traced back to the Bronze Age.

To perform lithomancy, stones are carved/painted with symbolic designs before being cast. The way the stones fall is interpreted to answer your questions. In some lithomantic traditions, diviners read the way that light reflects off the stones. In these traditions, colored glass stones are generally used instead of natural stones.

These are only some of the many forms of divination. Given the popularity of their form of magic, there are hundreds of variations of divination in the world. Some have their own sub-techniques and variations, which creates a potential list of thousands of divinatory traditions worldwide.

While mastering all forms is not possible, it is possible to choose the one which speaks to you the most – *and master it.* This book will help you explore astrology, numerology, palmistry, runic divination, Tarot card reading, and crystal divination in further detail.

Firstly, it will look at how astrology connects to divination and help you to understand what birth charts are and how you can make your own. Next, you'll learn about numerology and your life path number.

You'll then read about the Tarot, including an introduction to the cards and how to read them. Finally, the book will look at the following:

Palmistry

Runic divination

And crystal divination in further detail

By the time you have finished reading the book, you'll have a better idea of which of these relatively popular forms of divination speak to you most and which you'd like to explore further. You'll be able to make an educated decision on which form of divination to concentrate your abilities on.

So, what are you waiting for? All that's left for you is to turn the page and continue reading!

Chapter 2: Astrology and Divination

Astrology has been used for divination since the beginning of time. Several ancient cultures observed the positions of celestial bodies and associated their placings and movements with corresponding events that took place on Earth. Nowadays, while surrounded by many misconceptions, astrology is still one of the most popular methods for determining people's life paths. This chapter discusses the concept of astrology, its relation to astronomy, and how best to use it for divination.

The True Concept of Astrology

Astrology can be defined as a reflection of the connection between the activity of heavenly bodies and events surrounding people's lives on Earth. Astrologers study how planetary bodies affect one's career, health, and relationships. The latter can simultaneously be applied to more than one person, allowing the astrologer to analyze compatibility within a relationship. They can also predict how current global events, financial markets, social trends, and localized disasters are influenced by celestial movements. Because this is based on the movement of the planetary bodies within a specific timeframe, in-depth reports are usually generated weekly or monthly. However, astrology can also help predict more generalized pictures, which indicate possible future outcomes of one's actions. This is based on the placement of the planets at the time you were born.

While each celestial body has its own purpose in astrology, depending on the specific use of the reading, some are more significant than others. For example, personal readings always look at the position and the movements of the sun and the moon first, and then the other planets. This is because your sun sign determines your core identity while the rest of the celestial bodies influence smaller nuances of your personality and life. For a monthly report (used for horoscopes), astrologers only look at the zodiac sign a celestial body is currently moving through. They represent the final aspect of your personality. Together with the zodiac houses, they influence how your core personality is expressed.

Astrological Disciplines

There are more than 80 branches of astrology, each employing different practices, purposes, and subsets of techniques. However, most of them can be filed into one of the following categories.

Natal Astrology

As the most popular form of divination, natal astrology is based on the position of the major heavenly bodies at the time and date of your birth. This report is called the natal chart, a testimony to your predicted life path. It can be viewed as a blueprint of your life and used to examine what the celestial bodies gifted you with, including your strengths and weaknesses. As it allows insight into your soul's desires, it's often used to increase self-awareness. It helps you realize who you are, your most obvious personality traits, and what you can expect from your future. As mentioned, the prevalent factor to look out for here is your sun sign. However, plenty of other aspects can influence readings in natal astrology.

Horary Astrology

Horary astrology is an ancient divination technique that examines earthly events dating back to 30,000 B.C. It combines the use of the celestial maps created by ancient cultures and modern techniques, very similar to those used in tarot card readings. Despite requiring a look deep into the past, this branch can give you an incredibly accurate insight into future events. Astrologers create a chart specific to the location and the time a question is asked. By interpreting the chart, astrologers can provide "yes" or "no" answers to the question. If they run into a blockage, they can either assume that the answer is not yet ready to be revealed or take a different approach, such as consulting the ancient maps and repeating the question. Because it is so specific, this branch of astrology is practiced by skilled astrologers with a great deal of experience in extracting crucial details and fitting them into simple answers.

Electional Astrology

As its name implies, electional astrology involves choosing the most appropriate time for a particular event based on celestial action. Also called event astrology, this branch is used for planning events as well as predicting when some regular events may happen. It's great for accurately narrowing down the dates for positive occasions. If someone wants to know what astrology says about the best time of the month to go for a job interview, astrology can help them pick the right timing. Other advice that can be requested is when is the best time to meet a new partner, get married, or do anything else people may want to know. A person may choose to avoid an event by planning around retrograde movements of the planets or by looking at the moon. This luminary satellite affects your emotions, which may influence your experience at that particular event.

Mundane Astrology

Mundane astrology looks at the broad picture, examining global events and affairs. It has been widely used for thousands of years. Its origins can be traced back to a time when people were more interested in what the stars held for nations and their rulers. Like horary astrology, its mundane counterpart also takes past events into consideration. It examines patterns and looks at how the future may complete a cycle that began in the past. For example, each time the planets Pluto and Saturn meet, the inhabitants of the Earth experience events of historic proportions. And these events last until the planets start to distance themselves from one another. Mundane astrology can also be viewed as a unique form of birth chart for nations and historical events. Astrologers also use it to look at what happened at a specific time in the past and to predict whether or when it will happen again.

Medical Astrology

This particular branch of astrology links planets and zodiac signs to ailments affecting specific body parts. Planets are associated with organs or organ systems, while zodiac signs influence general areas of the body. This branch is a valuable tool for mapping out personal astrological charts. Astrologers can look at someone's chart and predict ailments the person might be afflicted by in the future. For example, if someone's zodiac sign is Leo, they're most likely to develop chest issues. If, when narrowed down to the planets, it's discovered that the chart shows Mars and

Mercury together in Leo, it indicates a possible heart condition in the future. That being said, these predictions are only to be used in conjunction with regular checks with health care providers.

Relationship Astrology

Probably the second most popular branch of astrology, divination related to relationships, is a unique discipline. While it's commonly used for determining compatibility in a romantic relationship, this branch can also be applied to any other type of relationship, from family to friends to work. Synastry is a specific form of relationship divination that directly compares two people's birth charts. The astrologers place one chart over the other and look at any overlapping positions of celestial bodies, zodiac signs, and houses. It helps to see where each person's strengths and abilities to support and relate to each other lie on a day-to-day basis. The composite astrological chart, or relationships chart, looks at the midpoint between the planets for each person, creating a third chart just for their relationship. After placing the two charts on top of each other, the position of the planets and signs are located. Then midpoints between all bodies that do not overlap are also determined. These points are then copied onto a new chart. This helps the astrologer predict the relationship's future and how it will be influenced by celestial actions.

Astrology vs. Astronomy

Since astrology and astronomy are both concerned with planets and other celestial actions, it's not surprising that they have common origins. In fact, back when people didn't make distinctions between science, culture, and religious beliefs, they were considered one and the same. Archeological records show that the terms astrology and astronomy were used interchangeably in ancient times. They represented a unified approach to the study of the sky, and astrological observations were made to improve astronomical predictions. This was the prevailing concept until modern sciences - physics and modern astronomy - showed us the importance of studying how celestial bodies affect each other and not just how they affect life on Earth.

Nowadays, scientists on both sides acknowledge a clear distinction between the two sciences. Modern astronomy is only concerned with the positions, properties, and movements of objects that exist outside of Earth's atmosphere. Astrology, on the other hand, is geared toward discovering how all these objects affect what's happening on Earth. While predictions of celestial phenomena are also employed in astronomy, these are only for scientific purposes.

Using Astrology to Predict the Future

The role of Divinational Astrology lies on several pillars. The most important ones are the position of the celestial bodies and the links between the zodiac signs and their original constellations. Based on this, we know that each moment in time represents a crucial part of an astrological chart. Astrologers can uncover insightful information about someone just by looking at their birth chart. A person's inherent values and qualities determine how they will experience the most significant events in their life. However, astrology can still not predict the future. It will not tell you the exact time of day you can expect to experience something. It only suggests an approximate time based on your actions and personal traits. You can use it to uncover potential opportunities, challenges, conflicts, and life paths. It can help you make meaningful choices about your future. Still, the outcome will depend entirely on your current and future thoughts and actions. If you suddenly change your mind and start thinking and acting differently from how you did at the time of the reading, the outcome may differ drastically. The celestial events can help you predict what the change may be. However, only a very detailed chart can help you reveal how the interactions of the planets and the zodiac signs will influence your life.

The Role of the Zodiac in Astrological Divinations

The term zodiac refers to the cycle completed along the ecliptic. As the sun travels across the sky, it passes through several stellar constellations. These constellations split the celestial ecliptic into twelve equal parts called zodiac houses - elliptical zones linked to the twelve months of the year. The zodiac is the oldest system designed to coordinate the placements and movements of the celestial bodies. The sign rules the month a person was born and their character. It may also indicate they have certain traits to use to their advantage or improve. By consulting your zodiac sign, you access information that helps you make smaller choices.

Ways to Have More Accurate Readings

In their eagerness to learn what the zodiac and the planets may hold for them, many people make mistakes that lead to incorrect readings and misleading information about future events. There are layers to an accurate prediction; the key to getting a clear picture is peeling off all these layers. Below, you'll see what this means and how it helps you do more accurate readings.

Use Full Natal Charts

The best way to access accurate information is to learn everything about the person you're reading for. This means exploring their sun, moon, and rising signs. Remember, the sun signs (the zodiac signs) represent only a small portion of the information pool you can find out about a person. Using only this reduces the chances of fully understanding someone's potential. For better results, create a chart using the person's specific birth location, birth time, and birthdate. This will allow you to create a more comprehensive astrological profile.

Pay Particular Attention to the Ascendant

The ascendant, or rising sign, shows how your personality is likely to be viewed by others. Although how people recognize you is a superficial element in astrology, it still carries weight. How a person interacts with their environment is coded into their core personality, giving you indirect access to it. It's also the fastest way to access crucial information about someone; you don't have to analyze how they think or behave - others have already done this, *even if they do so subconsciously.* Analyzing their opinion will save you considerable time. The ascendant also shows how a person moves through their life. This allows you to predict their future patterns and behaviors more accurately. Once again, it's important to use accurate birth information. The ascendant is the middle of the horizon at the time of birth and sets the basis of the entire chart.

Consult the Moon

Another way to find accurate information about someone's personality is by exploring their feelings. Emotions are ruled by the moon, and learning more about them can reveal someone's true potential. Developing emotions is related to the growth of one's inner world. In fact, how a person develops emotions towards their environment says more about them than how they act and speak. The moon also affects people's ability to nourish their relationships. While this information may contradict what the sun sign says about a person, it's often more accurate.

Improve Compatibility Readings

Their sun sign tells you very little about a person's relationship compatibility. Just as it won't give a clear picture of someone's personality, it won't let you see their value to others. Because relationships are built on common values and the ability to respect other people's values, even if they differ from yours, you'll need to look at the full charts of all people in the relationships you're analyzing. This way, you'll see what works and what doesn't. A person can work on accepting another person's values, but they'll rarely abandon their own. Improving your compatibility readings is also good practice for developing more in-depth personal charts.

Don't Rely Too Much on Retrograde Motion

Despite their challenging nature, retrograde transits are sometimes given too much importance. There is nothing wrong with wanting to avoid their negative impact, but sometimes this isn't possible. In addition, focusing only on what retrograde motions bring could prevent you from predicting small but positive changes. Instead, focus on these helpful signs. By recognizing them, you'll be able to steer the person concerned clear of any mishaps during retrograde. For example, you can plan to avoid anything that involves communication when Mercury is in retrograde. However, instead of trying to avoid making a mistake by evading communication with everyone around you, you can try to make the best of what life offers during the retrograde and focus on expressing your thoughts in other ways.

The Astrological Chart Wheel

General astrology charts can help you interpret several aspects of life, including past patterns, a group's behavior, or a person's nature. This allows you to make more precise predictions about the future related to the subject in question. The astrological chart wheels contain the symbols for the ruling sign and its polarity, the ascendant, the ruling zodiac houses and their opposites, and the placement of the planets. Here is how to decode an astrological chart wheel.

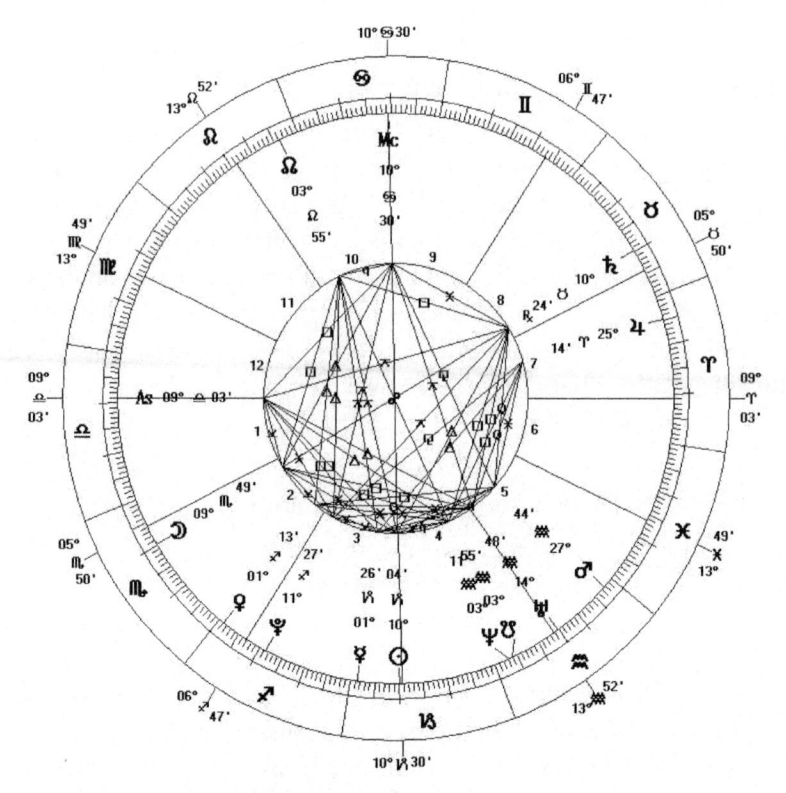

Astrological chart wheel.

Maksim Attribution-ShareAlike 3.0 Unported (CC BY-SA 3.0) <https://creativecommons.org/licenses/by-sa/3.0/deed.en> https://commons.wikimedia.org/wiki/File:Astrological_Chart_-_New_Millennium.JPG

Locating the Zodiac (Sun) Sign

The 12 zodiac signs, or sun signs, reflect the sun's annual journey across the sky. The symbols and polarities of the signs are as follows:

- ♈ Aries - ♎ Libra
- ♉ Taurus - ♏ Scorpio
- ♊ Gemini - ♐ Sagittarius
- ♋ Cancer - ♑ Capricorn
- ♌ Leo - ♒ Aquarius
- ♍ Virgo - ♓ Pisces

Learning about the Houses

Locations are based on the position and trajectory of the earth as it rotates around its axis over 24 hours. Here are the ruling houses and their opposites, as seen on the chart:

First I - Seventh VII
Second II - Eighth VIII
Third III - Ninth IX
Fourth IV - Tenth X
Fifth V - Eleventh XI
Sixth VI - Twelfth XII

Understanding the Planets

Here are planets affecting a chart. They are divided into personal planets (like the sun, the moon, and Mercury) and outer planets (all the other planets).

☉ **Sun** - Responsible for self-esteem, confidence, self-image, and sense of identity

☽ **Moon** - Shapes the values, emotions, and intuition and provides an emotional compass

☿ **Mercury** - Rules over communication, the ability to research and collect information

♀ **Venus** - Influences art, relationships, passion, pleasure, money, and beauty

♂ **Mars** - Prompts action and increases tension, expression, courage, and sexuality

♃ **Jupiter** - Responsible for luck, abundance, and prosperity

♄ **Saturn** - Creates boundaries, rules, limitations, and discipline

♅ **Uranus** - Allows breakthrough, rebellion, and sudden changes and events

♆ **Neptune** - Involved in spirituality, intuition, and developing compassion and ideals

♇ **Pluto** - The Planet of rebirth, death, transformation, and power

Aspects

The aspects of the chart determine how the different positions are related to each other. Here are the symbols of the common ones:

☌ Conjunction

⚼ Sesquiquadrate

⚺ Semi-sextile

⚻ Quincunx

✳ Sextile

☍ Opposition

□ Square

△ Trine

∠ Semi-Square

Other Points and Symbols

Another pertinent symbol in astrological symbols is the ascendant, which is the sign ascending on the eastern horizon at the time of a person's birth. Apart from this, other points may be presented, depending on how detailed you want to make the chart. Here are some other symbols you might encounter:

☊ North Node

Mc Midheaven

☋ South Node

Vx Vertex

℞ Retrograde

⚷ Chiron

⚳ Ceres

⚵ Juno

⚴ Pallas

⚶ Vesta

Chapter 3: Decoding Your Birth Chart

Your natal chart can give you insight into your life's purpose. This map shows the available paths, areas of abundance, and possible problems you may face. Since it is a map, learning to read it can give you all the guidance you need about where to go and what you need to do to get there. Your birth chart is your go-to guide for self-growth and development. It highlights all the qualities you need to work on and the areas you need to pay attention to throughout your life's journey. A natal chart outlines your life's purpose and how you should go about it.

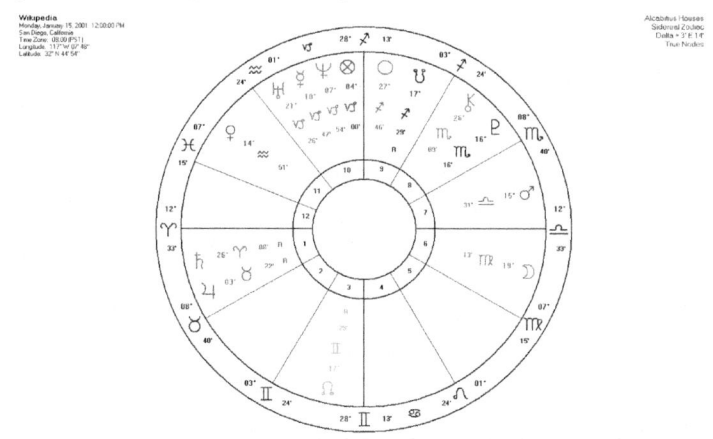

Your natal chart can give you insight into your life's purpose.
https://commons.wikimedia.org/wiki/File:Wikipedia_Sidereal_Birth_Chart.gif

What Is a Birth Chart?

You can think of your birth chart as a 2D map or screenshot of what the sky looked like at the exact time and place of your birth. If you can't read a birth chart or at least gain a basic understanding of it, it will probably look like a confusing collection of lines and symbols. This is why learning to decode your birth chart can be a bit intimidating at first. Natal charts speak their own language, and it takes a decent amount of time, energy, and dedication for them to start making sense to you. However, putting in the effort is well worth it. You can make a free birth chart online using your date of birth, time, and place of birth.

The Time of Birth

The planets and the stars are constantly on the move. Everything in the sky is always in motion. Whether we realize it or not, the sky looks different each minute. If you are plotting your birth chart, it is essential to know the exact time of your birth. You might not know the exact time of your birth, but there is sure to be a family member who will know.

Don't be discouraged if no one seems to know your birth time. You can use an estimate. Look up the exact time of sunrise on your date of birth for a sunrise chart. You can also use a noon chart - just put in 12 p.m. You can always seek the help of an expert astrologer too! They can give you an in-depth reading of natal chart rectification. This means that they'll ask you specific questions about your life that can help them uncover your birth time.

The Location of Birth

At this moment, the sky looks different everywhere in the world. The sun sets and rises at different times, and the constellations appear and disappear in different places depending on where you are in the world. This is why birth location is another crucial piece of the puzzle. The location of birth accurately determines what the sky looked like at the time of your birth, and it says a lot about your character and personality.

It Is Where You, Time, Earth, Space, and the Sky Meet

Most online charts generate a wheel or circular birth chart. However, some traditions may depict it in the shape of a square (or other shapes).

One thing you need to know about reading a birth chart is that you shouldn't read it by looking at it from above. Birth charts are read as if you are right in the center of a 3D construction. This can be confusing because the directions are then flipped. If you're using a regular compass, West would be to the left and East to the right. North is up, and South is down. However, when reading a natal chart, your East is West, and your North is South.

Why Are Birth Charts Significant to Divination Practices?

What benefit would be gained if you learned that Mercury makes a trine to your Neptune or that Uranus is square to your ascendant? Mastering the art of decoding birth charts can't be done overnight. So, is it really worth the hassle?

If you're already active in divination, then you're probably already aware of just how comprehensive the study of Astrology is. It touches upon every aspect of your life, allowing you to discover who you really are. It teaches you all about your core needs, desires, and motives in life and provides insight into who you are meant to be.

Your birth chart uses the language of stars and the positions of the planet to dive into your psyche. It's a way to find out what you're capable of and how to take a step closer to unlocking your full potential. Analyzing your natal chart helps you learn about your talents. We're not only referring to musical, athletic, or artistic endeavors, but we're also talking about one's soft skills. Astrological charts also identify people's weaknesses. Whether you have trouble controlling your anger or go into a self-destructive mode when you're stressed, decoding your birth chart can help you learn more about yourself and make the changes necessary to heal or control these weaknesses and capitalize on your strengths.

If you learn how to use it correctly, you'll get to know yourself so much better in every area of your life, and you'll soon be able to share your knowledge with others. With practice, you'll be able to do readings for your close friends and family, which will also teach you a lot about them. You'll begin to understand the things that make your loved ones feel uneasy. You'll know to look at the moon for answers when you want to know what makes someone feel safe and secure. You'll immediately navigate to your Venus if you wish to explore your love language.

You can improve your relationship with anyone by studying their natal chart. It helps you understand how they approach their relationships, what they look for in friends and partners, what they respond to, and how they express their love. Even if you're both completely different or if you have disagreements, learning about that person can help you become more empathetic and compassionate toward them. When you find out what motives and desires they're driven by and what their core needs are, you'll come to know why that person behaves, feels, or thinks the way they do. This also applies to your relationship with yourself. Instead of criticizing your actions, you'll grow to appreciate yourself and surround yourself with people who appreciate you.

Birth charts can be an incredible tool whenever you need to patch things up after getting into a conflict with someone. For instance, if you tell your friend off for being extra moody, you'll become more understanding once you find out they're a Scorpio moon. Scorpio moons are usually very sensitive to the vibes around them. They can easily take in both bad and good energy, which makes it hard for them to control their moods. A Scorpio moon could be having the best day ever before it all turns upside down when they interact with a friend who feels down.

Studying someone's birth chart reveals their natural patterns. You could also compare both of your charts to find out if your energy matches theirs. Learning that each of you expresses yourself and approaches conflict differently will help you to put things into perspective. It reminds you to take a moment and pause whenever you feel angry or confused about any aspects of your relationship. Birth charts are significant to divination practices because they dive deeply into several aspects of one's personality and being.

How to Decode Your Birth Chart
Before We Start

What Is the Ascendant?

Your ascendant or rising sign can be found in the Eastern hemisphere on the left side of the chart. It's called the rising sign because this is where the Sun rises. The degree of your ascending is that of the rising at the time and location of your birth. This is the point that most deeply and closely represents you.

What Is the Midheaven - MC?

The Midheaven or MC is basically the Southern hemisphere on your birth chart. It is the high noon and is when the Sun reaches its highest point in the sky. It is representative of your general image and professional success.

What Is the Descendant - DC?

The descendant is where the sun sets in the Western hemisphere. It is representative of your relationships and interactions.

What Is the Imum Coeli - IC?

The Imum Coeli is the midnight of your birth chart and can be found in the Northern hemisphere. It has everything to do with your inner life.

Birth Chart Components

The planets, the aspects of the planets, the signs, and the houses are the four core components of the birth chart.

Planets

Our motives and drive are represented by the planets. For instance, the drive to love and build intimate connections with people is ruled by Venus, while Mars represents the drive to win and succeed. Traditionally, our main focus in the birth chart is the planets we can see from Earth with just our naked eye. Mars, Venus, Saturn, and Jupiter can all be seen by the naked eye, along with, of course, the sun and the moon. Now, with the help of modern technology, we can add Pluto, Neptune, Uranus, and minor celestial bodies. The following are the roles of the planets:

Sun - Represents your identity and how you stand out.

Moon - Rules our emotions and bodies.

Mercury - Associated with how we communicate and where we do it.

Venus- Deals with how we connect with others and where we do it.

Mars - Related to how we take action and in which areas of life.

Jupiter - Linked to how you create abundance and where you'll find/create it in life.

Saturn - Represents our boundaries, how we create them, and where we do them.

Uranus - Related to how we innovate and think out of the box.

Neptune - Associated with how we use our imagination and the areas where we use it the most.

Pluto - Rules over how we possess our secret power and where we hold it.

Aspects

Aspects are representative of the relationships between the planets. They're just like us. Some planets get along, while others don't work well together. Some have neutral relationships, and a few don't deal with others at all. If you work toward self-awareness and put in the effort necessary, you can get all the planets to make peace with each other. Instead of a challenging birth chart, you can end up with one that is supportive and helpful. The following are the traditional aspects:

Gifts

Sextiles: planets that are 60 degrees or 2 signs apart are called sextiles. For instance, one planet can be in a fire/earth sign while another lies in an air/water sign, respectively. Since these planets work well together, sextiles are considered gifts. However, they are a little less intense than trines.

Trines: Planets that are 1/3 of a full revolution apart - planets that are 120 degrees or 4 signs apart. These planets co-exist harmoniously and communicate seamlessly. They bring protection, comfort, and blessings into your life.

Challenges

Squares: planets that are 3 signs apart are called squares. For instance, a planet that falls in Scorpio and another in Leo would make a square. These planets are a bit harsh, and they urge you to take action. They cause points of friction.

Oppositions: planets that are 6 signs apart are called oppositions. As the name describes, these planets lie in signs that are opposite to each other, which is why they're the most challenging. Whenever we feel overwhelmed, we need to find a way to create a balance between those opposing forces. We are encouraged to take a moment to think about what we offer to the world and what we must take from it.

Mergers

Conjunctions: planets that lie in the same sign as another are known as conjunctions. The closer those two planets are, the more their energies will amalgamate, generating unique traits and properties.

Signs

The signs represent how the planets express themselves. They guide the planet's mood, manner, and style of expression. The following are the 12 signs and each of their styles:

Aries: Action-driven, self-determining, and independent

Taurus: Grounded, sensible, and stable

Gemini: Conversational, intrigued, and curious

Cancer: Emotive, sensitive, and caring

Leo: Entertaining, charming, and expressive

Virgo: Analytical, observant, and perfecting

Libra: Justice-seeking, adaptable, and accommodating

Scorpio: Pervasive, perceptive, and mysterious

Sagittarius: Positive, cheerful, and hopeful

Capricorn: Self-controlled and disciplined

Aquarius: Intellectual, decisive, and definitive.

Pisces: Creative, innovative, and sensitive.

The signs serve as the planets' residences. According to traditional astrologers, the 7 planets we can see with the naked eye build unique relationships with the signs. Some planets thrive in some signs and, conversely, feel extremely uneasy in others. The signs also play another role. They divide the natal chart's 360 degrees into twelve 30-degree parts. Since the chart symbolically represents the sky to help us grasp a better understanding of it, the zodiac signs are also a symbolic reference to the constellations that are traversed by the sun from our perspective on Earth. This path is called the ecliptic.

Since these are all symbolic depictions, they're not all accurate. For instance, the constellations don't really make up twelve parts of 30 equal degrees. Take Virgo and Libra as an example: the former is twice the size of the latter. However, the birth chart serves the purpose of any other map. It aims to make things easier for us to grasp.

Houses

There are 12 houses, each representing a different area of life. The following are the different houses and the different areas that they govern:

The 1st House: Vitality, life, image and appearance, body, and self.

The 2nd House: Assets, belonging, income, resources, and living

The 3rd House: Communication, interactions, routine, daily life, relatives, and siblings

The 4th House: Parents, structure, essence, and home.

The 5th House: Creative endeavors, pleasure, intimacy, sex, and children

The 6th House: Health and professional life

The 7th House: Romantic partners, partnerships, and other commitments

The 8th House: Mental health, the resources of others, and death

The 9th House: Education, travel, spirituality, philosophy, religion, publishing, and astrology

The 10th House: Public image or role and career

The 11th House: Community, society, friends, good fortune, and sponsors

The 12th House: Sorrow, sadness, loss, secrets, mysteries, and hidden aspects of life

Even though the solar system determines which planets lie in the different signs, the "houses" depend on the moment and place of your birth. You may still be confused between the planets and the houses. Here's a trick to help you distinguish between both:

The moon is the fastest-moving celestial body. It takes around 2 or 3 days to pass through a sign. However, it only takes 24 hours to pass through all the houses in the natal chart. This is the same for all planets, as well. For instance, it would take Pluto anywhere between 12 to 32 years to make it through just one sign, while it takes only 24 hours to traverse all the houses.

How to Use a Birth Chart

Find an online tool to generate your birth chart.

You may be asked to enter your name, date of birth, time of birth, and location of birth.

Don't overwhelm yourself by trying to make sense of the entire chart at once. Start by observing the big three: your Sun, Moon, and rising signs. These will help you learn a lot about who you are.

For the coming three months, select one sign to focus on for an entire month. Meditate on the planet or the sign's aspects and think about how you relate to it, how you embody its energy, and how you wish to do it.

Keep a special birth chart notebook where you can journal all about your revelations and mental notes.

Even though you now have a better idea of what all the components of the natal chart mean and the roles that they serve, putting the pieces together can still be a challenge. It will take time until you are able to give an accurate birth chart reading. However, the learning journey is incredibly interesting and satisfying. Once you master the art of birth chart reading, you'll discover that you've unlocked a new language of expression; the language of the stars. You'll understand things about yourself that you've struggled to make sense of for years. Your life's purpose will suddenly become clear right before your eyes. The paths you are destined to take, the lessons that you need to learn, and the ways in which you need to grow and develop will all make more sense to you.

Chapter 4: Numerology

Numerology takes the numbers that are apparent in the world around us and applies them to our path through life. Think of numerology as a universal language but instead of using words, it uses numbers. In numerology, numbers have an energetic influence on people's lives, just like astrology and how the planets' alignments can impact your personality. Numerology can help you learn more about yourself, the world around you, and the people in your life. It is based on the theory that if you break down the universe's system, you will be left with the basic elements. These basic elements are *numbers*.

1.	2.	3.	4.	5.	6.	7.	8.	9.	10.	20.	30.	40.
A.	B.	C.	D.	E.	F.	G.	H.	I.	K.	L.	M.	N.
50.	60.	70.	80.	90.	100.	200.	300.	400.	500.	600.	700.	800.
O.	P.	Q.	R.	S.	T.	V.	X.	Y.	Z.	I.	V.	HI.
900.												
HV.												

Agrippan method of numerology.
https://commons.wikimedia.org/wiki/File:Agrippan_numerology_table.jpg

This may sound a little complicated for some people, as many usually associate numbers with mathematics. Most people take numbers for granted. Like the air you breathe, you don't think twice about its importance or what it means. You just inhale and exhale. However, numbers are much more powerful than you can imagine. On a cosmic level, numbers are considered symbols with strong, energetic vibrations that impact each and every person in the world. That said, not all numbers carry the same vibration; each number is unique, and so is its impact on individuals. Each number's vibration has its own properties, giving you an idea of your main characteristics and compatibility with potential romantic partners. Numerology can also help you discover your lucky day and lucky number. In numerology, everything happens for a reason, and this reason is numbers.

Everything related to you is made of numbers. Take a look at your birthday. It is made of numbers. Although your name is made of letters, these letters correspond with certain numbers which define who you are and impact your life's path. The same applies to your phone number, address, salary, etc. There are numbers everywhere around you and deep inside of you, so it makes sense that numerology will affect your life in different ways.

Numbers can affect your destiny as well as every part of your life, including your personality and certain life events. Numerology and astrology are deeply linked – numerology also deals with all the large heavenly bodies (the major planets) in our solar system (including Neptune, the sun, and the moon). There are usually two planets that govern your birth date, one primary and one secondary. Each person gives out vibrations of the planet and numbers associated with their name and birth.

Learning numerology can be overwhelming since there are various ways to navigate through it. However, having a background in astrology will help get you started, as it means that you are already familiar with numerology. In fact, you'll find more than a few similarities between the two subjects. Although Astrology and Numerology can help you gain more insight into yourself and the world around you, each uses its own method. Numerology works by calculating the numbers that make up your date of birth and the numbers associated with every letter in your name.

The History of Numerology

Numerology is an ancient study, and its origin is quite a mystery. Similar to many ancient philosophies, no one knows exactly where numerology originated. Some people believe that the Babylonians and ancient Egyptians first used numerology. There is evidence that shows that Japan, China, Rome, and Greece also used numerology during ancient times.

However, most people in modern times believe that the Greek philosopher and mathematician Pythagoras was the one whose theories most influenced the study of numerology. For this reason, he is often referred to as the father of numerology. No one knows for a fact whether it was Pythagoras or someone else who invented numerology. Just like the origin of numerology, Pythagoras's life remains a mystery, but his passion for numbers is a well-known fact. His mathematical theories have changed the way people in the modern world regard and treat numbers.

According to Pythagoras, numbers are extremely powerful in that they govern the world, and everything in life can be translated into single digits. Each letter is assigned a number which is called the Pythagorean Number System. This system is one of the fundamental bases of modern numerology. People use this system in different areas of their lives; however, in modern times, people use it the same way they use astrology to help them better understand themselves and to predict the future.

During ancient times, people believed that there were real powers behind each number. They also believed that the essence of the divine could be found in numbers, which could help them learn about God and themselves. This was when the oldest known form of numerology, the Chaldean System of Numerology, was used. In the Middle East and Asia, the study of numerology focused on the numbers in religious texts and their impact on people's lives.

Numerology and Astrology Combined

Numerology and astrology use different methods, yet both can help you better understand yourself and the world around you. Astrology studies the influence of the planets' positions on people's lives to help them find their true purpose in life. It also employs the power of the horoscope to predict the future. On the other hand, numerology uses various numbers associated with your life which can help you uncover information that will guide you in life. As mentioned, numerology uses your birthdate and name to create a chart, and astrology and numerology share the same foundation, which is mathematics. You need numbers to calculate the positions of the stars, their angles, and degrees at the time of your birth. Most people see astrology as a tool that helps you understand your personality and predict the future. However, you can't get there without mathematics. Since mathematics is all about numbers, this means that astrology and numerology can be interconnected and create a study that is referred to as astro-numerology.

You can combine the two to reveal your unique personality traits and pave your path through life. In fact, Pythagoras combined the two by associating stars with numbers. He later discovered that the two were very much connected since the planets, stars, and numbers were all intertwined. When combined together, both subjects can be much more powerful. That said, you don't have to be an expert in astrology to perform a numerology reading. All you need is to have an idea of every planet and its influence. Each number from 0 to 9 is ruled by a planet, the moon, or the sun.

Zero is ruled by Pluto

One is ruled by Sun

Two is ruled by Moon

Three is ruled by Jupiter

Four is ruled by Earth

Five is ruled by Mercury

Six is ruled by Venus

Seven is ruled by Neptune

Eight is ruled by Saturn

Nine is ruled by Mars

The moon, sun, and planets are connected with the energy and vibrations of each number. Using the combination of the two arts, one can get a deeper and more insightful look into their personality and life path.

The Various Origins of Numerological Systems

Throughout history, there is clear evidence that Many cultures used numerology. There were two methods that were commonly used during these times: Kabbalah Numerology and Chaldean Numerology. Later Pythagoras developed his own method, which is called Pythagorean Numerology, and people still use it to this day. Understanding the different methods of numerology will help you with your reading. Choose the method that you can understand and feel connected with. It is recommended that you stick to one method to avoid confusing yourself, especially if you are a beginner.

The Pythagorean Numerology System

Pythagoras was a Greek Philosopher and Mathematician who is often regarded as one of the fathers of modern mathematics. He developed his famous theorem when he was studying musical instruments and discovered that they vibrated at different levels – each of which he could attribute to a different number. The theorem he developed from studying music changed geometry as we know it and, importantly, showed a connection between the physical world and numbers. We can use Pythagoras's theorem to gain deeper insights into our lives and futures.

With the neurology system from Pythagoras, we can connect letters to numbers and use the letters revealed from dates of birth and names at birth to generate a series of numbers that can reveal our fate. Each person's name has its own number, and if a person decides to change their name, they will get assigned a new number. A person's name impacts their nature and personality; if they change their name, their nature and personality will most likely change as well. The idea of changing a name may be confusing in modern times. However, this is a tactic that Pythagoras used to change a person's destiny.

In the Pythagorean Numerology System, the basic vibrations begin from the numbers one to nine. While the master vibrations are numbers 11, 22, and 33. Master numbers should not be taken down to individual digits.

This method works with six types of numerology numbers:

Birthday number

Personality number

Power number

Attitude number

Soul number

Life path number

The Chaldean Numerology System

This system shares the most similarities with astrology. In fact, the Chaldean Numerology system and Western astrology both originated in Mesopotamia. The Chaldeans were an ancient group of people from Babylonia. They were intelligent people and knew that thoughts and words could influence the energy around people. The Chaldean Numerology system does not differ very much from the Kabbalah system of numbers or the Vedic system. You'll find a range of number systems across the globe that are all very similar in nature. The Pythagorean Numerology System differs a little and uses all the numbers from 1 to 9, while the other systems regard 9 as a sacred number and do not include it. Each letter has its own unique vibration, and each number has its own energetic quality, so letters are assigned to any number from one to eight.

The Chaldean system also has master numbers: 11, 22, and 33, and as with the Pythagorean system, they should not be reduced to a single digit. When the two systems are looked at, the Chaldean is the older of the two, suggesting that the Pythagorean system borrowed from it. But while they are similar in essence, they differ in how they calculate a fate or future, so they should not be used interchangeably. Individual digits are used to discover personality and traits. On the other hand, double-digit numbers can help uncover a person's inner personality, the deeply private one. When using the numbers to calculate from a name, the Chaldean system derives social status from the first name, the energy of the soul from the second, and self-image from a surname.

The Kabbalistic Numerology System

A system of Hebrew letters used to interpret people's names - it contained 22 vibrations. The Greeks and the Romans later adapted it into their own alphabets. Later in the 13th century, an interesting discovery was made as more people began using the Kabbalah system. They believed that God wrote the Old Testament using a secret code, and numerology was their best option to interpret the code and decipher its secrets. To a great extent, the twenty-two vibrations in this system also helped interpret the twenty-two tarot trump cards.

This method stands out from other Numerology systems as it only uses a person's name, but it doesn't use their birthdate, which makes it different from astrology which is based mainly on the person's birthdate. Numbers don't share the same values in different numerological systems. Even if the systems share similar methods, this doesn't guarantee that the value of numbers will be the same or give you the same results. It may not be easy for beginners to fully comprehend the Kabbalah system. This doesn't mean that it's impossible; it will just take you a bit longer. The system of Kabbalah has a central theme of balance and harmony, and there are between 1-400 integration paths depending on the unique vibration.

The Tamil Numerology System

The Tamil Numerology system is one of the most ancient numerological systems. This system originated in India, which is why it is also referred to as the Indian Numerology System. The Tamil system can give you a better insight into yourself so you can uncover your potential and learn about your abilities. You'll be able to look at the world in a different way and better see the path laid out before you. This system can deepen your connection with the world around you, especially during harsh times. It uses the planets' energies and their positions to help you learn about your personality and temperament.

The Tamil Numerology system focuses on the Name Number, Destiny Number, and Psychic Number in a person's calculations.

The Chinese Numerology System

As with most number systems, there are meanings associated with different numbers. And, within that, some numbers are luckier than others. In Chinese numerology, pairs of numbers are very important, and this theme of twos makes even numbers luckier than odd ones. Numerology also connects to acupuncture, and the body is divided by numbers, helping practitioners find points on the body depending on the number.

Angel Numbers and Angelic Numerology

This "angel/angelic" system is newer – especially when compared to some of the other numerology systems, and it does not have ties to the original systems of numerology, though it is influenced by them. It is believed that numbers have their own vibrations that can influence people. When taken further, the vibrations can be seen as created by design, and God created Angel Numbers as a way for heavenly beings to communicate. The most powerful numbers are the ones that repeat (have you ever wondered why we make a wish at 11:11? It can be traced to Angel Numbers). The same power comes in other repeated numbers and not just 11:11. Reading these numbers can help connect you with angels and reveal the divine powers and magic in your life.

How Numerology Can Deepen Your Understanding of Yourself

Consider numerology as a cheat sheet to help you figure out your true potential and uncover your inner self. Interestingly, the two things that are out of your control - your name and your birthdate - can influence who you are and how you live your life. Once you crack it using numerology, they contain a code that will help you discover your life's secrets. You have probably heard others saying that life would be much easier if people came with a manual. Well, you can consider numerology as a manual or guide that can help you learn about your various personality traits and better understand those around you as well.

Numerology has quite a number of uses. It can guide you toward finding meaning in your life and put you in the right direction. You can also use it to give you an idea of the kind of energy that will impact your life in the future. For instance, you can use numerology when naming your child since a person's name is extremely powerful and can impact their potential and personality.

You are often told who you should be or how you should act, either by your family, school, friends, or social media. Numerology is what can give you a great insight into your true potential and who you really are, away from all the outside influences and loud noise. Use this information to better understand yourself and improve your life. Similar to having a zodiac sign in astrology, in numerology, each person has a Life Path Number which can help them learn about who they really are and challenge them to answer life's most complicated questions.

There is a reason people have been fascinated with astrology for so long, as it can help them answer life's most difficult questions, such as who am I? Why am I here? Numerology can also help you solve the biggest mystery of all, yourself, and unlock your true potential. Using both subjects together can give you the answers you are hoping for.

Chapter 5: Your Life Path Number

Do you have a lucky number that you keep seeing in the strangest places? Each person has a life path number that is like their shadow. It is always with you wherever you go. You can see this number reflected in the things that inspire you; it gives you a sense of purpose and helps you to see your true life objectives. Your life path number, also called the destiny number in Chaldean numerology, is quite similar to your zodiac sign. You need to discover it to take advantage of all the information it offers. Many people often feel lost and struggle to find their place in the world, but armed with the information from your life path number, you'll find a sense of direction and grounding whenever life discourages or distracts you.

This number represents your core essence, which makes finding out what it is even more of a necessity. The art of numerology believes each person has a numerological destiny, and the key is your life path number. Aligning yourself to it will help you reach your numerological destiny and give you a better understanding of your life.

Each person has a life path number that is like their shadow.
https://www.pexels.com/photo/wood-nature-man-people-6806434/

Your life path number is any number from one to nine or 11, 22, or 33, which are referred to as master numbers. Just like zodiac signs, each of the basic and master numbers represents certain characteristics, weaknesses, and strengths. There is more than one type of zodiac sign - your sun sign and your moon sign - but the sun sign is usually the most significant. The same applies to numerology, and although there is more than one number in the numerological chart, no number is more significant than your life path number.

Your life path number helps you find your spiritual calling and uncover your deepest desire. For instance, if your life path number is two, this means that your spiritual purpose in life is to bring others peace. This prominent number can help you find the right career based on your skills, abilities, and personality. For instance, if your life path number is one or eight, you'll excel in jobs requiring leadership. However, if your life path number is two or three, you would be better suited for a career in the arts.

The Meaning behind Each Life Path Number

There is a special meaning behind each of the basic and master numbers. Before you learn how to calculate your life path number, you should first learn about the main characteristics behind each one to better understand your personality.

Life Path One

Life path number one individuals are known for their leadership qualities and independent personality. These natural-born leaders have the strength and determination to change the world around them. They have the qualities that are necessary to be great leaders, like originality, confidence, and independence. These individuals know how to achieve their goals and have the creativity to help them achieve anything they set their minds to. These people are destined to lead independent lives and learn how to stand on their own two feet without anyone else's help. You'll never find a life path one individual paying attention to other people's opinions or judgments regarding their lives. They are the ones who take the road less traveled. They lead an authentic and passionate life by being unapologetically themselves.

Their ambition is obvious in the way they go after their goals. They are willing to do whatever is necessary and have a clear vision and strategy that will get them there. They are risk-takers who don't hesitate when it comes to trying out new methods, even if they are dangerous or risky. They are not the type to walk away from something just because someone discourages them or tells them it isn't a good idea. They are brave enough to trust their gut and do things in their own way. In fact, this is usually how they achieve their goals. When this life path isn't in alignment, these individuals can be controlling, selfish, and extremely pragmatic. They can also struggle with overthinking and low self-confidence.

Life Path Two

These individuals are called peacemakers because of their understanding, gentle nature, and ability to mediate to restore peace. These peace-loving souls create balance and harmony wherever they go. It is essential for them to feel needed and loved by everyone they meet. However, love without respect is meaningless to them. In fact, they want to feel valued and appreciated for what they do. These people are great team players because they enjoy brainstorming and sharing ideas with other like-minded individuals. Whether it's their family or friend group, life path two individuals often act like a mother to all the people in their lives. They take care of their needs and provide for them.

If you have a life path two in your life, never lie or betray people with this life path because once you do, you'll lose their trust forever. These individuals are extremely devoted to their loved ones and emotionally sensitive. However, there are moments when they find their emotions overwhelming. They also often struggle with opening up and trusting others.

Life Path Three

It is very easy to feel drawn to the life path of three individuals. They have magnetic personalities, great communication skills, and are very charismatic. They find it easy to communicate with others and don't shy away from self-expression. They are emotionally sensitive, which is evident from how they treat everyone. Thanks to their extroverted nature, these individuals can easily make friends and are often the life and soul of the party. You'll find that they can achieve anything they set their minds to because of their confidence in their abilities and people skills. Although they are likable, and everyone seems to gravitate toward them, they sometimes find it hard to relate to other people's struggles. They don't like to show vulnerability or ask for help. However, maybe being vulnerable is what they need in order to relate to and connect with others.

Life Path Four

These individuals thrive in a stable environment. Hard-working and logical, they will do whatever it takes to achieve their goals. However, if they don't love what they do, they may struggle and fail. Because they are logical and dependable, their friends, family, and co-workers often come to them when in need because they know they can depend on them for support. They are realistic individuals who are focused on achieving their goals; they don't let anything or anyone distract them. They can be very stubborn and inflexible when it comes to their beliefs. It is impossible to change their minds.

Life Path Five

Life path five people are free-spirited individuals who are full of energy. They want to live an adventurous and free life without fear. In fact, freedom is their main purpose in life, so they often struggle with being committed to a person or place. They live life to the fullest and enjoy everything life has to offer; the good, the bad, and the ugly. This may make them seem indulgent and unpredictable, as they will do anything for the sake of a good adventure. Unlike life path four, these individuals can't stand routine or stagnation and thrive in change. They aren't the ones to stay in a job they hate and don't mind changing jobs until they find something they can be passionate about. Because of their adaptability, they can easily integrate into a new workplace.

These people need to be on the move, or they will feel stuck and suffocated. However, this can affect their relationships and make them seem selfish and irresponsible. Having an adventurous spirit can be an admirable quality as long as they remember that they have people in their lives that they can't neglect or leave behind.

Life Path Six

The aim of these people is to live selfless lives and to care for and nurture the people in their lives. They also have strong leadership skills, which is why they prefer to have their own businesses so they can be their own boss. They often act as counselors to their family and friends and manage to keep the peace. Life path six stands out as the least biased out of all the other life paths, thanks to its open-minded nature. They are fair individuals who just want to help others. These individuals can't tolerate injustice and are brave enough to speak up against it. As caring as these people are to those around them, it will benefit them to remember to look out for and care for themselves as well.

Life Path Seven

Just like cats, life path seven individuals are very curious and will do anything to satisfy their thirst for knowledge. They also want to lead a spiritual life focusing on their emotional side and intuition. Their heads are often in the clouds and tend to get caught up in what-if scenarios. They prefer to live with these scenarios in their heads than go out there and experience them in the real world. They spend their lives in search of the truth and are admired for their logical and creative nature.

These individuals are very sensitive and emotional. However, in a harsh world where sensitivity can be perceived as a weakness, they may feel like they don't belong and that they are different from everyone around them. This leads to struggles when connecting with strangers, often accompanied by overthinking situations and projections. However, they can control their overthinking by digging deep and finding ways to trust themselves and their abilities. Being different is nothing to be ashamed of. On the contrary, it should be celebrated.

Life path seven individuals need to give themselves a chance to discover who they are. When they connect with themselves, they can connect with others and develop real and deep relationships.

Life Path Eight

Life path eight individuals want to leave their mark on the world. Their motto is to "Go big or go home," and they have it in them to do this and anything else they set their mind to. Their goal is to succeed, and more times than not, it can be the only thing they focus on, which is why they tend to gravitate toward areas like finance or business. These individuals thrive when working in a team because they believe that working with others can help them achieve the success they very much desire. But their need to control everything can cause them to have trouble with anxiety. They need to relax, let go and believe that some things are out of their control.

Life Path Nine

Life path nine is the last of the basic numbers. Wise, creative, compassionate, generous, and humanitarian, they are the first to help those in their social circle and their community. These individuals believe they can make the world a better place through humanitarian work and connecting with other people. In fact, they inspire and motivate others to go out and help those in need and the less fortunate. Being selfless is an admirable quality. However, their selfless nature makes them so focused on others that they neglect their own needs. They may have trouble finding love because they are often afraid of showing how weak they think they are and letting others in. They shouldn't shy away from expressing their feelings and should remember to ask for help whenever they need it.

Life Path Eleven

The first of the master numbers, life path eleven individuals possess psychic abilities and strong vibrations. The goal is to find the ultimate path in life along with an equilibrium of the spirit and higher knowledge. These people are kind, helpful, and patient and use their special skills to inspire and help others. Just as they care about achieving a spiritual balance, they often inspire others to also go on a spiritual journey to discover themselves. Like everyone else, these individuals may experience unfortunate situations. However, they don't let anything bring them down and will often come out stronger than ever. This is why many people find them inspiring, and they also touch others with their kindness and big heart.

Life Path Twenty-Two

You know the saying that instead of giving a man a fish and feeding him for a day, teach him how to fish, and you'll feed him for the rest of his life? Well, life path 22 individuals believe in this saying wholeheartedly. They want to live a life where they can help others and make a difference in the world. However, they believe that the best way to make a difference in someone's life is by giving them the tools to succeed. People like this are persistent, happy, reliable, and full of wisdom. They are very creative and believe they can achieve anything they set their mind to if they harness their abilities.

Life Path Thirty-Three

Similar to other life path numbers on the list, these people live their lives to help others by using their healing and nurturing abilities. They want to make a difference in the world around them and be known as the loving and compassionate individuals they truly are. They are selfless, and there is nothing that they won't do to help anyone in need. At times, they can be so focused on helping others that they forget to be compassionate and end up being self-righteous and critical. If they manage to let go of their judgmental side, these individuals can be a force of healing in the world.

Calculating Your Life Path Number

You have gained insight into the numbers and what they mean. You can use this knowledge to easily find your life path number. All you need to do is keep adding all the digits in your birthdate until you get one single number. The following example will make things clearer and easier to understand.

For instance, your birth date is March 6th, 1992, 3/6/1992

Add the digits in the year to reduce it to one single digit. 1+9+9+2= 21. You are left with a double-digit, which means you must simplify them.

Take your two numbers and add them: 2+1=3.

Now, add the numbers that represent the month (3) and day (6): 3+6+3= 12.

You do not yet have a single-digit number, so you need to add the two digits together in the number 12: 1+2=3. Now, you have your number.

Always take the digits of any double-digit number and add them together before adding any other numbers to them. If the day or month are double-digit numbers, add them together before adding them to other numbers. However, if the results are 11, 22, or 33, don't add these numbers as they are master numbers and have their meaning in numerology.

Enneagram Number

The Enneagram number is yet another tool to help you better understand yourself. An enneagram is a psychometric assessment of your personality. It shares similarities with numerology since both can help you learn about your characteristics and personality traits from your birth date. However, the enneagram also focuses on how you behave or act in various situations throughout your life. For example, your behavior when you are stressed. There are nine personality types in the enneagram system, and like numerology, each type is associated with a number. The best method to find your enneagram number is by taking an online test. A simple online search will take you to various websites, many of which are free, where you can take the test and learn not only about your personality but your motivations to act a certain way.

If there is a person that you should know more than anyone else, it's yourself. However, most people struggle to understand themselves and find their true purpose in life. Discovering your life path number will help you discover your purpose. Calculating this number is very easy. Just keep one thing in mind. The number you calculate should be a single digit. If you have double-digit numbers in your date of birth (for example, the month is November (11)), you need to add them together before adding them to any other numbers. The only exception to this rule is when you are adding your final life path number and you get a double-digit number with the same number (like 22). These powerful numbers are left as they are and can be interpreted without being simplified. Once you learn your life path number, you can better learn about yourself and your place in the universe.

Chapter 6: The Divining Art of Tarot

The tarot has been used as a divination tool ever since the rise of mysticism in the 18th century. It all began in Italy during the late 14th century when the card game Tarocchi was invented. It had complicated rules and striking imagery.

Occultists assigned certain meanings to every tarot image.
https://www.pexels.com/photo/close-up-shot-of-a-person-holding-tarot-cards-7181711/

Cards like the Moon, the Sun, the priestess, etc., were initially adopted from Tarocchi. Moreover, as this game continued to gain popularity across Europe, society's elites commissioned artists to create personal imagery specifically for them. Often the knight of cups, the hierophant, and other figures was based on the family who hired the artist.

During the early 18th century, European and Western occultists drew a link between Tarocchi and an Ancient Egyptian text used by gypsies in Europe. These occultists claim that the Tarot originated in ancient Egypt. However, this claim has not been supported by real evidence to this day.

Based on their observations, occultists assigned certain meanings to every tarot image. Western occultists divided the Tarocchi cards into two groups, the Major and Minor Arcana. They noticed that the Major arcana, formally known as the trump cards, use Hebrew letters found in the Kabbalah, which are magical Hebrew interpretations of the Torah. These letters are connected to certain elements, planets, or zodiac signs. After this discovery, the Major Arcana gained more evolved, richer meanings.

As for the Minor Arcana, there were slight changes made. In the 1700s, the suits were different. Both traditional and modern decks contain similar suits (swords and cups), but modern decks have replaced staves and discs with wands and pentacles.

Every image holds secret messages and codes. The meanings behind these mystical images changes depending on which cards surround them. Since the changes were integrated into tarot, they have been used as a divination tool that informs the reader of the past, present, and future. People have been using it to answer unanswerable questions and ease their worries.

Types of Tarot Decks

The Tarot of Marseilles

By the 16th century, Marseilles, France, and Italy were the tarot hubs. Later, in the 18th century, Grimaud, a French company, published the Tarot of Marseilles, a deck that became all the rage across Europe. It gained so much popularity that the company started exporting this deck to other companies. Later, cities in northern Italy and countries like Switzerland and others started to print and publish this deck.

The Tarot of Marseilles is truly remarkable because it paved the way for the modern tarot. The 18th-century occultists based their theories on this deck, and the ever-famous Rider-Waite-Smith deck's design was based on the Marseilles deck.

The Rider-Waite-Smith Tarot Deck

The Rider-Waite-Smith tarot deck is one of the most famous tarot decks to this day. It was developed by Arthur E. Waite, designed by Pamela C. Smith, and published by William Rider in 1910.

During this time, William Rider wrote The Key of the Tarot, which was published with the deck. This book was a guide to help people interpret the tarot and learn the art of picking up its energies.

The Rider deck's popularity spread like wildfire, and every tarot practitioner was using it. Today, most modern tarot decks' designs are based on the Rider pack. Many practitioners today still use the Rider deck, whether on their website or with their clients.

The Thoth Tarot Deck

Aleister Crowley developed the Thoth Tarot deck in 1944. This deck follows hermetic principles and is connected to systems such as astrology, the kabbalah, and the golden dawn. This deck is perfect for readers who want to integrate different systems as they are conducting a reading.

Cultural Decks

Modern-day tarot is based on the Marseilles and the Rider decks. The idea behind them is the same as the previous decks, but their designs are completely different. The more tarot grew in popularity, the more freedom it gained.

Though the meanings remained the same, the designs rapidly changed. Why is this important? Imagery is a powerful tool. When people see pictures that they can relate to, the energy collectively changes. Tarot is energy work, so the readings are more accurate if the energy is intensified.

Cultural decks do not have a specific design, but when you see one, you'll recognize it. These types of decks are used by people from all different nationalities and ethnicities.

They often reference elements from various cultures, and these elements vary from cultural symbols to universal references that everyone can understand. The universally referenced images convey messages that help the card reader with their interpretations.

Oracle Cards

Oracle cards are slightly different from tarot cards, but they are used in the same way. These cards also have images and often have a message written on them as well. Oracle cards are used in conjunction with tarot spreads and often help the reader give a clearer reading or support what is seen in the tarot spread. Oracle cards are widely different from one another. You can find cards that are centered around the phases of the moon, seasons, elements, astrology, fairy folk, and different themes.

Which Deck Is Suitable for You?

There is such a wide variety of tarot cards available that it can get a bit overwhelming when you are buying your first deck because you want it to be special. Still, any deck that you buy will be special since it is the first of your ever-growing collection.

Every tarot reader has a personalized system and style. As a beginner, you probably haven't settled into your own style yet. This is just the start of your journey, and it will take a bit of time to get there, so there is no need to force anything. Readings are based on intuition and introspection, so when you buy your first deck, follow your instincts. Since there is no one way to pick your first deck, here are a few pointers that can help you when you are about to purchase your first set of cards.

Connection

One of the easiest ways to pick a deck is to see which one you feel connected to the most. Take yourself to the store and browse all the different cards. After you have finished browsing, check in with yourself. See which deck you feel attracted to the most or see yourself using more than the others. Gut feelings and intuition are powerful, so listen to them.

Pick a System

Certain Tarot decks are attached to different systems. For instance, the Marseilles and Rider deck are basic decks. They have a few astrological elements, but the rest is fairly simple. On the other hand, the Thoth deck is connected to the golden dawn, astrology, and the Kabbalah. If one of these systems stands out to you, then this is your sign to purchase the deck that is connected to it.

Google Them

Another easy way to do this is to Google the decks that interest you the most. You can see what they look like on the inside. If you are a visual person, then this method will help you. After you have Googled your cards, pick the ones that call out to you the most, and you can use your intuition to help you.

Size Matters

You'll have to do a lot of shuffling when practicing tarot, so make sure that you pick a size you are comfortable handling. Tarot cards vary in size, so check the cards' size before buying them. You want to be comfortable shuffling them, especially when you are a beginner reader.

Card Attunement

One of the most significant steps that you need to cover is card attunement. This is a process by which you connect your energy with your cards so that your intuition can pick up their messages, resulting in accurate readings. It is vital that you connect with your cards whether you are a beginner or an advanced reader. Whenever you buy a new deck, you have to connect with them. There are multiple ways that you can do so if you do not know how to connect to your deck.

Quality Time

Spend time with your cards. The more you are around them, the more your energy fields intertwine. This means holding them and setting your intention to connect with them. You can sleep next to them or cover them with a garment or a necklace that you wear often. You can keep them in your hands for a while or shuffle them a bunch of times.

Journaling

You can also journal and reflect on your new cards. Hold each card in your hand, then journal about them. Pick a random card and journal about the feelings that it inspires within you. You can also set your intentions when you are journaling. You can write about how you are feeling about your new cards and state that you are connecting with them. You can also note down how it feels to connect with your deck. Emotions are strong with tarot, so make sure you use your feelings when journaling.

Meditating

Meditation is another powerful tool that can help you to connect to your cards. Find somewhere comfortable, or go to your meditation place if you have one. Then hold the cards in your hands and begin breathing and meditating. As you inhale and exhale, imagine your energetic field connecting with the cards. Envision yourself using the cards smoothly and experiencing accurate readings.

Deck Cleansing

Your tarot cards are connected to your energy, so when this card energy has been used or tarnished, it needs to be energetically cleansed. Using your cards before they have been properly cleansed is going to compromise any reading you may make. Generally, it is best to cleanse the deck before and after every reading.

This cleansing is necessary because whoever you have done a reading for was channeling your cards energetically, and they could leave their energy attached to the cards. This means that when you are doing a reading for yourself or someone else, this person's energy will still be lingering, and that is never a good thing, so make sure to cleanse your deck.

You'll encounter difficult and deep readings with yourself and others. You might do a reading for someone who is going through emotionally challenging times. If this is the case, then make sure you properly cleanse your deck before and after this reading so that you do not take this heavy energy with you.

How to Cleanse Your Deck
Smoke

Any type of incense will work when you are cleansing your deck. You can also you can use herbal smoke. Aim to use cleansing herbs like sage, rosemary, peppermint, basil, and sweetgrass. You can also use palo santo to cleanse your deck from any unwanted energies.

Visualization

This may sound bizarre at first, but *visualization* is a powerful tool. Your mind and energy field are capable of so much more than you might think. All you need to do is put the cards in front of you, close your eyes, and imagine a bright golden light entering your deck and cleansing it from the inside out. After you feel like your cards have been purified, you can begin using them.

Crystals

Crystals contain powerful energy within them. Like herbs, each crystal has a different set of properties, so look for ones that have purification energy. You can use crystals like Black Obsidian, Selenite, Black Tourmaline, Smoky Quartz, Amethyst, Rose Quartz, Citrine, Clear Quartz, Turquoise, Sodalite, and so many more. You can place any of these crystals on top of your deck and pick them up later when you feel they have been purified.

Sound

Sounds and certain frequencies have purification abilities. You can surround your deck with beautiful music or use your signing bowl and produce sounds that purify the deck's energy. You can also sing to your deck, and it can be a beautiful part of your practice. Find something that matches your style and use whatever method you are most comfortable with.

Moonlight

You can also leave your deck beneath the Moonlight. The full Moon phase is the most powerful, so you can leave your deck beneath the Moon at its peak. However, any other Moon phase will do.

Sunlight

The sunlight has healing and cleansing energies. You can set your deck beneath the Sun and return to it when you feel it has been cleaned. You can also do this when your readings have been a bit fuzzy or unclear.

Salt

Salt is a powerful cleansing tool. You can drench your deck in sea salt or regular salt. You can also set salt stones on top of your deck and use them when they have been purified.

Tips and Tricks

Grounding

If you are a beginner tarot practitioner, then grounding yourself before a reading is necessary. The tarot functions by using the energy field of the reader, so if you are not centered, then your reading can drain you. On the other hand, your energy could be scattered and not focused, which will result in an inaccurate reading. A good way to ground yourself is to sit on the floor with bare feet, take deep breaths, and set your intentions for the reading.

Utilize the Energies

Grounding techniques are a big part of the reading ritual, but sometimes you'll need something stronger when you are unable to ground yourself. You can use different tools to help you with your energy field. Try reading in nature. You can be in a garden or on the sand; both will ground you. You can also use crystals. Let's say you want to preserve your energy as you are doing a reading. In this case, you can wear crystals that protect your energy.

Use the Baby-Step Method

Interpreting tarot cards is fascinating, but it can also be overwhelming at first. As a beginner, you may be confused or flooded by all the cards and patterns you need to learn. You can prevent this by easing yourself into the process. Learn about one card each day. You can set two piles down - learned and unlearned cards. The more your learned pile grows, the more you can try creating patterns and interpreting them together. You can also try the 3-card pattern first before you delve deeper into more complex patterns.

Learn Patterns

Speaking of patterns, you'll find plenty of spreads that you can create with the cards. There are classic ones like the Celtic cross, the 3-card spread, the 5-card spread, spiritual guidance, relationship, astrological, and so many more. You can ease yourself into this by learning easy spreads, like the 1-card reading and the 3-card spread. As you practice these spreads and get more comfortable, you'll be able to take on more elaborate patterns. Later, you can create your own patterns and inquire about the cards about anything you are wondering about.

Practice

The traditional tarot deck has 78 cards and numerous spreads. You cannot expect to learn all of this overnight. It needs time and a lot of practice. You'll gradually get the hang of it the more you learn - *and the more you practice what you have learned.* The best way to practice is by yourself. Try doing a lot of readings for yourself until your reading is smooth and your intuition is sharp. Then you can start giving close friends reading to test your skills with other people.

Learn from Others

The tarot is an ancient practice, and people have been practicing it since the 18th century. So, you can imagine how it has evolved and how people have found new ways to have more accurate readings. Get some tarot books and learn how different people read their cards. Adopt anything that evokes inspiration within you until you have developed your style.

Tarot is a divination tool that has been part of people's spiritual practices for years and has helped many people by answering questions and easing worries.

The beautiful thing about tarot is that anyone can practice it; it is not an exclusive practice. If you are thinking about becoming a tarot practitioner, you need to include it in your spiritual practice.

Purchase a deck that you feel connected to or attracted to. Then cleanse it and spread them so that you can get to connect with them on a more intimate level. Do not try to rush the process; ease yourself into it and familiarize yourself with your cards one step at a time.

Now, you can start learning one card a day and familiarize yourself with different patterns. This may feel slow at first, but do not be discouraged. Your pace will increase one day at a time. Eventually, you'll find yourself conducting readings for yourself easily. Remember to ground yourself before readings and cleanse your deck before and after your readings.

Chapter 7: How to Read the Tarot

Embarking on your tarot journey must feel exciting and overwhelming all at once. You do not have to worry about this, though, because this chapter will help narrow things down for you, and you'll find where to start and how to expand your knowledge when it comes to your new practice.

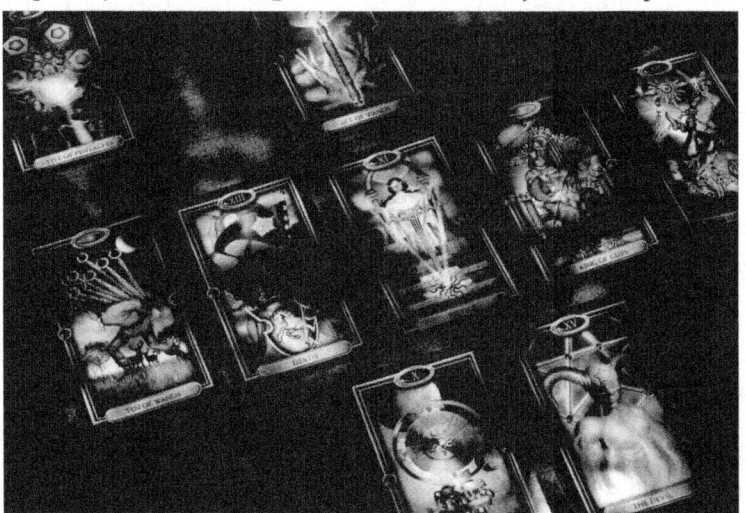

There are several placements that allow you to read tarot.

https://pixabay.com/es/photos/tarot-tarjetas-tarjeta-profec%c3%ada-2114403/

We have set out a few rituals that you may want to adopt. These activities will help you gain a fresh perspective, feel calm and centered, and put your mind in the right space to do effective readings. You may feel like there are a lot of rituals to remember and go through before you start reading, but you don't have to follow all of them. They are merely pointers to help you to have a clear reading, and it is really up to you to decide whether you would like to include them in your practice or not.

Remember, at the end of the day, tarot is a highly personal practice, which means that you get to decide what it should be like for you. You'll eventually have your own style, with your own set of rituals and ways of reading. So really, there is no reason to worry about the form of your practice. Just go with the flow, and you'll find that your practice has taken on its own form and shape.

Rituals

Almost every spiritual practice has rituals, and tarot is no different. Every practitioner has a routine that they go through before listening to the cards. And, since you are a new reader, it may be best that you are introduced to different practices to decide which ones you like and will use - and which don't resonate with you.

As mentioned in the previous chapter, grounding and cleansing are vital before reading. To recap, you can ground yourself by meditating, using crystals, or sitting with nature. You can also resort to other methods when you want to ground yourself. However, if you feel like your energy is scattered, then grounding is necessary.

Cleansing is also a must. This is a practice that you simply cannot disregard. You must eliminate any energy in your cards for a clear and accurate reading. Otherwise, your readings may be off-key, and the energy that has lingered on may affect you or others negatively, so be careful.

Intuition Tuning

Tarot reading is half an understanding of symbology and half intuition. And as a beginner, you might have some of the following questions. What does this mean? Have you ever seen a little book that comes with the tarot deck? Well, this book explains what each card means. However, why do we need tarot interpreters if there is a book that clearly explains every card? Why is it a spiritual practice? What is so special about this?

It is true that every card is clearly explained. However, that is not enough. Understanding the symbols is one thing, and interpreting the cards is another. Your intuition is the tool that helps you to decode the cards. Think about it, how will a book be able to explain different spreads and patterns with the cards that you drew out? A book cannot decipher this, but your intuition can.

There are various ways that you can sharpen your intuition. You can start by making meditation a daily practice. Meditation trains your mind to be quiet and listen to the subtle messages coming from your intuition.

You can also use essential oils to stimulate your third eye. Opening your third eye sharpens your intuition and helps you hear it. You can use lemon, jasmine, or sandalwood mixed with a carrier oil and rub it on your pineal gland. You can also inhale their aroma instead of putting them on your skin.

Crystals such as Rhodonite, Amethyst, Purple sapphire, Sodalite, Violet Tourmaline, and others can help clear the pathways between you and your intuition. You can spend time meditating with the crystal of your choice and setting your intentions to listen to your intuition. You can also carry these crystals with you to keep your intuition sharp. Remember, setting your intentions with spiritual work is everything.

Shuffling

Shuffling your tarot cards is a must. Firstly, it helps restore energy. Secondly, mixing the cards up as you focus your energy helps you get a good reading.

There is really no one specific way to shuffle your cards; you can do it however you like. Just remember to set your intentions and channel your energy as you do so. You can talk to your cards as you move them around. You might pose questions to the cards or ask for a reading.

Pick Your Cards

Usually, beginners have a difficult time picking out a tarot card. They are unsure how to do it and often doubt themselves and their intuition. If you have been going through this doubt yourself, know that it is okay and that it is a normal part of the journey.

Picking out your cards will get easier the more you practice. You can start by spreading them out after the shuffling. Ideally, they should be faced down when they are spread out. Now you can start connecting with your intuition and feelings. Try to feel which cards are calling out to you. The cards you feel most attracted to are the ones that are supposed to be in your reading.

Spreads

By now, you are familiar with tarot spreads or patterns. However, to paint a clearer picture, this section will explain what spreads are and the types of patterns that you can use.

To put it simply, a tarot pattern is a way of placing the cards chosen in a certain manner. For instance, one card can be on top of four other cards. This is one of the five-card spreads that you can use. You can put three cards next to each other, and this is known as the three-card spread.

The Celtic Cross

The Celtic Cross is one of the most popular spreads. It features ten cards, each representing a different element or factor. So, begin by shuffling your cards while focusing on your question. Then spread the cards and pick ten of them.

The first card should be placed in the center. This card is called the querent, and it represents you.

The second card should be placed horizontally on top of the first card, creating a cross. It is called the block. From the name, this card represents the problem or the situation that is stopping you.

The third card should be placed beneath the central card. This one is known as the root. It identifies the cause of your problems.

The fourth card should be placed next to the left of the central card. This card is known as the recent past, and it shows you what has been taking place lately in your life.

The fifth card, or "Possibilities," goes above the central card. It represents different options or possibilities around you in the present.

The sixth card goes next to the right of the central card. This represents where you are going or where you are headed based on your present situation. It can also show you what you need to do to achieve the desired outcome.

To place the seventh card correctly, imagine there is a line forming next to card six. Add card number seven at the bottom of this line. This card represents how you see yourself and your power in the present moment.

Place card number eight on top of the seventh. This card represents your current environment and the kinds of influences that might be affecting you right now.

The ninth card goes on top of the eighth. This card will reveal your feelings, hopes, fears, and everything in between.

Finally, the tenth card goes on top of the ninth. This card will give you a picture of the outcome based on the current situation.

Three Cards

The three-card spread is one of the simplest patterns that you could use. Usually, beginners practice with this pattern because it is the easiest to use, and it introduces them to the concept of patterns in general and how they can use more complex ones.

Basically, any three cards next to each other is a three-card spread. You can ask the cards about anything and pick out three cards that will give you your answer. Here are a few sample patterns, but remember that you can create your own.

Situation, Action, Outcome

Yes, Maybe, No

Past, Present, & Future

Embrace, Accept, Let go

You, the Person in question, the Relationship

The problem, Cause, Solution

Mind, Body, Spirit

Other Patterns

Spreads are endless in tarot. There is really no one way to do it, and readers continue to create their own patterns every day. You can make up any variation that you think will best fit your question. Here are a few spreads that you might like:

Relationship Spreads
Four Cards

Your feelings

Other person's feelings

Relationship pros

The future of your relationship

Six Cards
Current Situation
Reasons to stay
Reasons to leave
Your feelings should you stay
Your feelings should you leave
Advice

Career

Five Cards
Dream job
Path to dream job
Your unique qualities
Assistance
What should you focus on right now

Six Cards
Your goal
Your challenges
What is it taking from you?
What is it adding to you?
What does your job give you?
Factors that affect you

Shadow Reading

Ten Cards
What is my shadow self like?
What are you trying to communicate to me?
What am I blinded to?
How do I ignore your messages?
How can I heal you?
When were you born?
Which lost part of me do you represent?
What are you trying to teach me?
How can I understand myself better through you?

Interpretation

Traditional Reading

Traditional reading means sticking to what everyone knows about tarot and using that to figure out what the card means. If you would like to read the tarot traditionally, then you'll need to do a lot of reading and learning. Look for different books written by authoritative authors and soak up their knowledge. Take note of how they interpret the cards according to the traditional way.

The drawback of this kind of reading is its lack of flavor. It is not original and is empty of style and identity. Sticking to traditional tarot can ease your worries about interpreting the cards correctly, but this way, you'll be erasing your own voice from the reading.

Intuitive Reading

Intuitive reading means interpreting the tarot by listening to your intuition. Intuitive reading does not ignore the traditional meanings of the cards. On the contrary, it takes them into account. However, it does not rely heavily on the traditional meanings of the cards. The best way to do an intuitive reading is to mix the traditional meanings with your intuition, resulting in an accurate and spiritual meaning.

This kind of reading can be tricky at first, but the more you are in tune with your intuition, the more you'll be at ease when reading. You will notice that your confidence reaches new heights the more you practice.

Symbols

Symbology is key in Tarot. Pick any random card right now, and you will notice various symbols on one card, whether it is a lake, moon, chains, lantern, castle, etc. You can read your cards by interpreting the symbols they have. This goes into intuitive reading because it is not enough to rely on symbols alone. Still, symbols are powerful when properly understood.

You need to be well-read to understand the different symbols. You can try to learn a few symbols every day and note down your newly found knowledge so that you do not forget. You can check out these symbols in your tarot books or be aware of the popular symbols around us.

Reversed Reading

Have you ever noticed reversed cards in a tarot reading? There is a reason these cards are flipped, but the message really depends on the interpreter. If you want to experiment with reversed cards, you need to intuitively flip a few cards here and there and then shuffle the whole deck. This will result in a few reversed and upright cards.

Now you can begin picking out your cards and interpreting your cards. You'll read the reversed cards in the same way you read the upright ones, just in reverse. For instance, the hermit represents chosen solitude, soul-searching, inner guidance, and inner wisdom. When it is in reverse, it means isolation, pushing others away, and loneliness.

Additional Tips

Tarot Journaling

Keeping a tarot journal will become a powerful tool in your arsenal. The more you write down your readings or take notes from them, the more confident you'll become in your craft. You'll be able to see a pattern of how your intuition works, which will make you trust it even more. This habit also allows you to connect deeply with your craft. Being connected to your tarot deck makes your readings more powerful and soul-felt.

However, be careful that no one else touches your deck if you plan to build this deep connection with it. Energy work is subtle yet powerful. You do not want anyone else's energy to have a negative impact on your energy or your deck.

Tarot and Oracle Cards

Now, this area is completely up to you - but you can mix tarot cards with oracle cards. You can do this by shuffling your tarot deck and picking out as many cards as you see fit. Then shuffle your oracle cards and place them near your tarot cards. Then you can begin to interpret what the cards are telling you.

This mix gives you more insight and more room to interpret things that you did not see before. The more room you give the cards for them to speak to you, the louder they will be. So, try it out and see if this is something that helps you or if you would like to include it in your craft.

Mix Your Decks

Mixing your decks is similar to adding oracle cards to your tarot reading. You can do this by purchasing a couple of decks that have attracted your attention. Then, after you have finished cleansing them and connecting with them, you can mix them together.

Shuffle each deck separately, then pick out as many cards as you like from each deck. Proceed to read them together. How does this help?

Well, each deck offers different imagery and various symbols. This can help you to see underlying factors that you have not seen before, and this will give you more insight.

After you have finished, make sure you thank the cards and put them back in their original deck. Be careful not to mix them up together, and, of course, cleanse them once you have finished using them.

Ambiance

Creating an ambiance for yourself helps you get in the zone. For instance, if you are used to reading with soft light and music, then every time these elements are around you, you'll find yourself focused and centered.

You can have incense, candles, or crystals around you. You could have a tarot table set up in a section of your house or a whole room that is dedicated to your readings. You can read in nature or indoors. It is really up to you, but whatever you choose, make sure that it enhances your focus and calms you down.

Reading the cards is not as complicated as it seems. It might seem like a lot at first because there are 78 cards in one deck and a lot of patterns that you'll need to learn. You'll have to learn the meaning of each card, as well as what it means when it is surrounded by different cards. There is absolutely no reason why you should not feel overwhelmed at first. The learning journey is rich with new knowledge that you'll have to soak up to become a practitioner.

However, your intuition is a powerful tool that makes the learning journey much easier than it may initially seem. Sharpen your intuition as you learn new meanings and decipher various symbols. Do not forget to practice grounding and trust your intuition because it will help you read with clarity and accuracy.

Finally, do not be afraid to mix it up. This is a personal journey, and it is only natural that you develop your own unique style when you interpret the cards. So, it is really up to you if you want to include different tarot decks or oracle cards in the same reading. You cannot have a "wrong" style when it comes to this beautiful and spiritually insightful practice. Happy readings, dear tarot reader.

Chapter 8: Palmistry and Palm Reading

It's human nature to be curious about the unknown, particularly about what the future holds in store. This curiosity has led to the invention of numerous predictive sciences and techniques. Divination techniques like numerology, astrology, and palmistry have always attracted people, whether in days gone by or in modern times. Palmistry, or the art of palm reading, is an ancient technique that helps determine one's personality traits and possible predictions of what their future holds. Also sometimes known as chiromancy, the art of palm reading is not bound to a singular culture, religion, or region. Instead, it has moved all over the world, passed down from generation to generation. Due to its origin, the practice has many versions used to analyze the various lines and features displayed on the palm of a hand. A palm reader is a name often denoted to those who read the patterns in palms, and a palmist is also a given name, but the actual name for someone who dabbles in the art is a *chirologist.*

Palm reading requires attention to the details found in the lines and groves.
https://pixabay.com/es/photos/mano-l%c3%adneas-cauce-palm-piel-5219349/

Out of all the divination practices, the art of palm reading is considered the most highly regarded, although it's a bit challenging to master. Hands, particularly palms, are seen as valuable portals that can shed light on a person's characteristics and even predict their future. There are a few factors to weigh in to make the complete analysis. However, understanding the basics of palmistry is not as difficult as you might think. And once you learn the ropes of this powerful predictive technique, you'll be on your way to mastering this art in no time. This chapter will provide a detailed guide to palm reading, its history, theories, and techniques.

History of Palmistry

There's a general uncertainty about the origins of palmistry. While many people believe that it originated in India and spread elsewhere from there, others argue that it was started in ancient Greece by the great scientist Aristotle. The art was then passed on to Alexander the Great, who took a keen interest in the subject and practiced it in the hands of his soldiers. Moving further into the future, Hippocrates also employed palm reading techniques to diagnose diseases. While it may have started in Ancient Greece, it soon spread to India, China, Persia, Egypt, and many more countries.

The rapid spread of this divination method can be attributed to the fact that people were fascinated by the thought of predicting the future, and with so many predictions being accurate, there was no shortage of believers. Today, palmistry is still as widespread as before, if not more so. Modern palmists often relate their readings to psychology as well to provide a more in-depth analysis.

Palm Reading Guide

Although there are numerous versions of palm reading techniques all over the world, there are some steps and theories that are followed universally. A good chirologist thoroughly analyzes every line, feature, mount, bump, and intersection on the palm. While a simple analysis can be made by identifying and interpreting the major lines, a more thorough reading would require you to study the shape of the hand, identify the different mounts and what they represent, and finally, interpret the meaning of the major and minor lines and intersections present on the palm. Furthermore, you should also characterize the shape and size of each finger present on the hand and make classifications based on the color of the palm.

Choose a Hand

Before you can start interpreting the meanings behind various features present on the palm, you need to select a hand to analyze. For women, the right hand is considered to be what you're born with, whereas the left hand portrays your accomplishments throughout your life, and, for men, the opposite is true. Some prefer selecting your dominant hand as a representation of the present and past, while the other hand represents what is to come.

Opinions on this subject vary, but most experts believe that it's necessary to analyze both hands to reveal the natural personality and future potential. The readings reveal how a person is and how they can use their characteristics and potential in this lifetime.

Determine the Shape of the Hand

The human personality is a pretty complicated mixture of characteristics and attributes. Similar to how astrology classifies various attributes with the time and place of one's birth to elemental signs, palmistry also relates the four elements with one's hand shape. Each hand type directly correlates with one of the four elements: water, fire, earth, and water. However, your astrological or birth chart readings may not always align with your palm readings. So, even if you have a fire sign in your birth chart, the shape of your hand may reveal you to be a water sign, which may signify the complex nature of your personality. Each hand shape has specific features and traits associated with it, as listed below:

The Earth Hand

Like the earth, they are firmer and more solid. The palm is more or less a *square shape*, with short fingers. The skin of the palm is thick, tough, and ruddy in color. Palm length and finger length are roughly the same. People with earth hands are practical, energetic, responsible, and humble. They are usually good leaders and great at managing people and executing instructions. Earth hands show people who are to be relied on and offer security – they do not become absorbed in themselves and their own problems and are a person who can be leaned no in times of need.

They are not very ambitious at times and are usually comfortable with a moderate lifestyle and basic necessities. Jobs that require minimal complex operations are most suitable for these people. They're not the kind to make grand romantic gestures; they are happiest with simple romance. Those with earth hands can develop breathing ailments and are not great with heights.

The Air Hand

Air hands are not fleshy and have more squat palms that are not as round as other elements – the skin is often dry. This hand type signifies intelligent, curious, and smart individuals who are good at analyzing situations and adapting to change quickly. They have an innate desire to explore things and are often gifted with a highly creative side. People with air hands yearn for a romantic lifestyle and are usually social butterflies. This leads air hands to be less focused than others, and if they do not have enough stimulation in life, they can become bored or on edge.

The Water Hand

These hands are longer and lither – both the palm and the fingers. Longer fingers generally lead water hands to be players of instruments. Water hands are softer than their counterparts, and they can be oily or clammy too. They know how others are feeling and often feel the same. Water hands are in touch with feelings, intuition, and seeing beyond the physical realm. These individuals are fueled by kindness and creativity. Mostly introverts (though there can be exceptions), people with water hands are very emotional and get hurt easily. This can cause some personal stress and issues. Their interest is in all things beautiful and creative; thus, many are huge art lovers.

The Fire Hand

Fire hands have lengthened palms with shorter fingers. The fingers are usually shorter in length than the palm. The palm itself has a pinkish or ruddy coloring with defined mounts and creases. Traits associated with fire hands people include an energetic nature, smart, diligent, optimistic, and self-confident. People with fire hands are usually extroverts by nature and are often the life of the party. These individuals love a colorful life and never let a moment get dull. However, they can be somewhat lacking in compassion and may make bad decisions driven by their desires.

Identify the Mounts

Identifying the type of hand is only the beginning. The next step is to study the palm in more detail. You are looking for the mounts – the fleshy areas on the palm. We can look to the planets for more information on our mounts.

The mounts that seem rounded and elevated represent the stable nature of the attributes associated with the respected mount. Whereas sunken mounts depict the individual's weaknesses or vulnerabilities in regard to specific attributes. Furthermore, mounts that are extremely prominent or elevated reveal a person's dominant traits, which can impact their lives and personality positively or negatively. To observe your mounts, cup your hand just a little and notice which ones are protruding and which ones are not.

Outer Mars, Inner Mars, and Plain of Mars

You cannot look at palms without utilizing Mars. Mars is the planet (and god) of war, and you'll find aggression, resilience, and temperament in the mounts when you read them. Look for the Inner Mars above the thumb, and use the mount to discover the strength of the individual. You'll also find the Outer Mars on the palm, and this will tell you the persistence and emotional intelligence of the individual. Finally, the plain of Mars, which lies at the lower center of the palm, signifies how the qualities mentioned above are balanced together.

Mount of Jupiter

Look to this mount for passions, dreams, confidence, and authority. It is located at the base of the index finger, right above the inner Mars region. The mount itself signifies a connection to the divine and the spiritual realm. If this region is prominent, it shows that you're dominant, confident, and maybe somewhat arrogant. If this region is lacking, it means you lack confidence.

Mount of Saturn

Located at the base of the middle finger right next to the mount of Jupiter, this is associated with wisdom, intelligence, fortitude, and responsibility. This region exposes whether or not a person has integrity and the ability to take responsibility when things get bad. A too-prominent mound shows that you're stubborn and cynical. And, when there is not a mound, the person is shallower and more unorganized.

Mount of Apollo

Find this mount under the ring finger and beside the Saturn mount. Apollo (the sun) relates to happiness, optimism, and vigor. The Apollo mount also shows the artistic side of a person and their potential in life. If the sun mount is excessively prominent, it means you're extravagant and quick-tempered. A low mount means you lack imagination and creativity.

Mount of Luna

The mount of Luna is located at the end of the palm, towards the side of the pinky finger. The name comes from the moon goddess, and you'll find empathy, knowledge, wisdom, creativity, daydreams, and divination in this mount.

Mount of Mercury

The mount of Mercury is located right below the pinky finger and is attributed to an individual's wit, charm, social skills, and adaptability. This region represents if the individual is resourceful or not and how their mind works strategically. If it's protruding, you talk too much. A lack of a mount of Mercury can signify shyness.

Mount of Venus

Look for this mount at the root of the thumb. You'll use the mount of Venus to discover the sexuality, sensuality, and amorous nature of the person. The type of mount will show how drawn people are to the person and how deep of a connection they can form.

Identify the Major Lines

The most important aspect of palm reading is interpreting the palm's folds, creases, or lines. While numerous lines are present in the palm of a hand, only the main ones are the focus for narratives and predicting future happenings. Several features come into play when focusing on the major lines. Their length, curvature, and depth all make a difference in the final interpretation. It's crucial to observe minute details of the lines, where they begin and end, where they intersect, and which mounds they cross.

Each of these details plays a part in the complete interpretation of a reading.

The Life Line

Located above the mount of Venus or the base of the thumb, the life line is the one that arches slightly and extends around the thumb. Contrary to popular belief, the length of the life line does not predict how long you'll live. Instead, it reveals your health and physical fitness. The depth of the line depicts the fullness of your experiences, whereas the length reveals the influence of other people on your life. The life line can be displayed on one's palms in the following ways:

A large arc that is on full display - the individual is full of life and vibrancy

A long life line - signifies the person's physical fitness and athletic nature

A slight arc toward the base of the palm - the individual might have fatigue often

Multiple life lines - meaning the individual is full of life, optimistic, and happy.

The start of the life line is frayed (near the wrist) - signifies the early life sickness a person might have had

The end of the lifeline is disrupted or broken (near the index finger) - the individual should pay attention to their health problems when they get older, as they are likely to face issues

Circle, spiral, or cut in the life line - the individual might get physically hurt

A straight line moving across the palm - an individual who is courageous and confident

The Heart Line

The heart line, or love line, is located across the palm, right under the fingers. It can be slightly arched or move straight horizontally. The heart line reveals attributes related to the heart. These can include feelings, emotions, love, lust, romance, and emotional control. The heart line is usually observed on the palm in these ways:

Straight and small - someone who is closed off from love and relationships

Lengthy line across the palm - an understanding person when it comes to relationships - they will treat others with care

A line that touches the index finger - the outlook for love is positive

A line coming into contact with the middle finger - someone who is more self-absorbed and will be like that in a relationship.

A heart line ending between the ring finger and middle finger - someone who is quick to engage in romantic relationships

A line with a lot of movement (not straight) - someone who engages in short relationships with many lovers

Circles on the heart line or broken heart lines can denote unhappiness in a relationship

The Money Line

You'll find the money line (or fate line) between the middle finger and the wrist. Also referred to as the line of destiny, this line reveals how much a person's life will be influenced by external factors out of their control. Our hands, especially our palms, will change over time, which means that our fate will change too. It represents an individual's career or fortune. The following cases can be observed for the fate line:

A life and money line that starts together - a person with a lot of confidence and believe in themselves

Double fate line - an individual with an entrepreneurial spirit who takes on more than one job at a time

Simple, straight line - a fortunate or lucky person. The person is lucky in terms of careers/money

A split money line - someone who feels the need to switch jobs or roles frequently

A short line - a person who might retire before retirement age

The Head Line

Our minds play an essential role in shaping our destiny. Thus, the head line reflects a person's intellectual capabilities and pursuits. It lies in the very center of the palm and might arc a little. Look to the head line to discover what you need to learn in life to make the best of it. You'll also find signals of intelligence here, and the line will offer insight into a person's educational pursuits and what they might pursue. Different head lines will denote very different things:

Wavy lines denote more progressive thinking and ways of adapting

Straight lines are straightforward, just like the person. They want to take the easy path through life (not in a bad way) and stick to what they know

A cut in the line can denote mental suffering or pain that needs to be broken through

Large curves in the line shows great creativity

When the head line is short, it shows a focus not on educational pursuits, and the person is more likely to find success in physical pursuits

The Marriage Line

An important line to pay attention to when completing a full reading, but a line that is often ignored, especially when the person is not in a committed relationship. It is a short line located right above the love line. It starts right under the pinky finger. The marriage line reflects a person's romantic relationships and married life. Some people have just a single marriage line, while others have multiple lines above the love line. Simply observe the clearest one.

A double marriage line - someone who might engage in multiple relationships at the same time

Several marriage lines, none clear and distinct - the person may not be happy in their married life

A short or barely visible line - it might take some time for the person to wed

A longer line and almost starches to the pinky finger - a person who has high standards when it comes to what they expect from a relationship

A line that touches the ring finger - indicates money will be abundant within a relationship

Circles or gaps in the marriage line - the couple may have to live separately for a while

If the line is split in two, it shows a potential break in the relationship, and the relationship will need extra care and attention

Although palmistry has been a long-practiced form of art, it does not yield exact answers and might not always be accurate. So, as you familiarize yourself with the various theories and features of palm reading techniques, don't lose hope if you don't get pleasant results. The real purpose of these readings is to help you get lessons regarding your life so that you can channel your energy into working harder for those parts.

Moreover, let your intuition guide you when making the interpretations, and keep in mind that both hands and people can change with time. Palm readings aren't set in stone, so think of them as a way to develop insight to select the best way to move forward.

Chapter 9: Runic Divination

Runic divination is also an ancient method for predicting the future. Runes are long associated with Vikings, and they found their origin in the Scandinavian countries and also some Germanic areas. Runes were to the Vikings what the alphabet is to us, and the runic alphabet predates the Latin alphabet. During the Middle Ages, these nations used runes for recording important events, accessing spiritual wisdom, and more. The word "rune" means "secret" or "mystery," alluding to the symbols' ability to reveal information that's only understandable by people with a strong intuition. This chapter is dedicated to runic divination, discussing its history, the use of runes, the different runic alphabets, and the interpretation of runic layouts.

The use of Runes dates back to the time of the Vikings.
https://pixabay.com/es/photos/runas-adivinaci%c3%b3n-runa-magia-4267425/

History of Runic Divination

Runes have a long-standing history. Norse legends confirm that the god of wisdom, Odin, discovered the runes during his ordeal at the Well of Fate. He then taught them to other deities in the Norse pantheon, which in turn, passed them onto mankind. The symbols were collected into an alphabet named Futhark, after the first two letters of the runes of the alphabet. The symbols were etched into wooden sticks, which the tribe's spiritual leaders then used as tools for accessing wisdom, protection, and strength.

Apart from being a letter in an ancient alphabet, runes also represent a universal force affecting people's lives, shaping their destiny and life path. Some are linked to the Norse gods and goddesses themselves, giving the seeker access to ask for guidance during divination. While the meaning of the runes may have slightly changed over time, they are being used to predict future events and outcomes.

How Can You Use Runes?

Runes can be used to reveal what happened in the past, what is happening around us, and what will come to be in the future. While they won't give you exact answers, they suggest how to proceed. Just like tarot cards, the reliability of the results depends on how you interpret the runes and what you decide to do after receiving an interpretation. This means that whatever answer you're looking for, you'll need your intuition to decipher it from the runes.

Since the future isn't fixed, you can also use runic layouts to change undesirable outcomes. If you're reading for yourself and you don't like the suggested result, all you need to do is change your aspect. You can do this by doing a deeper reading and learning what the best course of action is likely to be. Make the change, and the next time you do a reading, the suggested outcome will be different too.

Runic divination can be particularly helpful in situations where you have limited access to information about a possible future event or circumstance. Consulting the runes allows you to get the full picture - as long as you listen to your intuition.

Different Types of Runes

Originally runes were made from a branch of a nut tree, cut into specific lengths, and marked with symbols. Nowadays, runes are made from wood, stone, metal, bones, crystals, and pebbles. You can buy them along with a storage pouch and the white cloth they are traditionally tossed onto during the reading.

There are also different symbols or alphabets. The oldest one was called the Elder Futhark - and was in use from at least the 3rd century, although it's possible it was used even before that. This alphabet had 24 symbols divided into three Aetts or families - Freyr's Aett, Heimdall's Aett, and Tyr's Aett. Later, this alphabet was switched to the Younger Futhark, which only had symbols. Another version, the Anglo-Saxon Futhorc, had 33 runes - and it was an adaptation, so it could be translated to Old English.

The Meanings of Each Runic Symbol
Elder Futhark

Freyr's Aett:
Ruling over fertility, peace, sunshine, and peace, this aett shows you how to stay grounded in the material world.

Fehu ᚠ - Translated as "cattle" or "wealth," fehu is associated with abundance, hope, luck, and prosperity. Apart from material gain, it can also indicate good social status.

Uruz ᚢ - Translated as "ox." The ox is strong, brave, resilient, has vitality, is persistent, and works hard. The ox rune can signify health in an individual.

Thurisaz ᚦ - Known as the giant or Thor's hammer, this rune represents a challenge, protection, and power to direct one's energy to destruction, defense, or even cleansing if needed.

Ansuz ᚨ - Translated as "message," this is the rune of revelation, communication, insight, messages, signs, wisdom, inspiration, and knowledge obtained from divine or spiritual sources.

Raidho ᚱ - Also known as a journey, this rune indicates progress, evolution, and perspective. It could be interpreted as traveling physically or as a spiritual journey.

Kenaz ᚲ - Translated as "torch," Kenaz is the rune of knowledge, enlightenment, calling, ideas, and comprehension. It may also indicate the truth that's waiting to be revealed.

Gebo X - Known as "gift" in modern English, this rune denotes generosity, gifts, assistance, or talent that you either possess or will be given in the future.

Wunjo ᚹ - A rune of protection and security, especially within a group. It can denote luck, success, prosperity, and celebration.

Heimdall's Aett:

Named after the guardian of the gods and wisdom, Heimdall's aett indicates maturity and the ability to overcome obstacles and persevere despite them.

Hagalaz H - Translated as "hail," this rune represents destruction, uncontrollable forces, the power of nature, and disasters. It also indicates inevitable and necessary changes.

Nauthiz ᚾ - Translates as "needs." The needs rune symbolizes desires, needs, survival, denial of satisfaction, arguments, restrictions, and not enough.

Isa I - Isa is the ice rune and is about patience, taking time, pausing in daily life, and delay. Just as ice blocks a stream, the rune can show a blockage of a life.

Jera ᛃ - Translated as "harvest," Jera is the rune for a conclusion, end life cycle, beginnings, growth, plentiful bounty, and the abundance of wisdom.

Eihwaz ᛇ - Known as "yew" in English, this rune symbolizes connection, sacred wisdom, and divinity. It's also associated with the cycle of life and The Tree of Life.

Perthro ᛈ - Perthro can be translated as "destiny." The rune represents fertility, female energy, fate, good fortune, mysteries, chance, and influence.

Algiz ᛉ - Translated as "elk", this rune symbolizes protection, awakening, instincts, and guardianship. It often prompts you to tap into your internal power to reach your goals.

Sowilo ᛋ - The symbol of the sun, Sowilo represents vitality, success, joy, happiness, cause for celebration, or even good health and the results of reaching your goals.

Tyr's Aett:

The aett of the Norse god Tyr represents justice, war, legacy, intuition, birth, and celebration.

Tiwaz ↑ - Translated as "victory," Tiwaz symbolizes leadership, bravery, rationality, honor, and courage. It indicates that you're capable of persevering in troubling times.

Berkana ᛒ - Berkana is the birch rune, and symbolizes fertility, birth, creativity, renewal, coming together, and new beginnings.

Ehwaz ᛖ - Translated as "horse, "Ehwaz denotes moving forward, trust, progress, loyalty, duality, animal instinct, and the need for assistance.

Mannaz ᛘ - The symbol known as "man." It represents humanity, collective spirituality, relationships, mortality, values, and identity.

Laguz ᛚ - Translated as "lake," this is the symbol of water, dreams, imagination, mystery, insight, psychic and healing abilities, and knowledge.

Ingwaz ᛝ - The rune of Fertility, Ingwaz is the symbol of variety, virtue, peace, inner growth, family, ancestry, well-being, and loose ends tied up.

Othala ᛟ - Also known as "heritage" in English, this symbol represents inheritance, legacy, values, contribution, finding out what truly matters, and communal prosperity.

Dagaz ᛞ - Translated as "dawn," this rule indicates a new day, awakening, a sense of clarity, hope, a new cycle, increased consciousness, and the possibility for a breakthrough.

Younger Futhark

Here is the meaning of the Younger Futhark runes. This list contains the 16 runes used in the first version of the Younger Futhark.

ᚠ **Fé:** Translated as "wealth," this rune symbolizes money, finances, and wealth. It can be the cause of many conflicts between family members and friends.

ᚢ **Úr:** Known as "iron" or "rain" in modern English, this rune denotes an unexpected event. It can be positive, as a blessing, or negative, as danger.

ᚦ **Thurs:** Translated to English as "giant," this rune symbolizes the Norse god Thor, who was known to be a giant person with brutal force.

ᚨ **Ás or Oss:** This rune literally means "one of the Æsir" (or gods). It denotes divine order, absolute truth, and divine justice.

ᚱ **Reið:** Known as "ride" in modern English, this rune symbolizes a spiritual journey. It's applied for raised awareness and spiritual growth.

ᚲ **Kaun:** Best translated as "ulcer," this rune means that one must first endure suffering to gain wisdom.

ᚼ **Hagall:** Also called "hail" in English, this rune denotes a sudden and unclear change or outcome.

ᚾ **Nauðr:** Translated as "need," this rune also signifies distress or difficulty in persevering in challenging situations.

ᛁ **Ísa or Íss:** Known as the rune for "ice," this is a symbol of self-control and the ability to remain calm.

ᛅ **Ár:** Translated to English as "plenty," this rune denotes plentiful harvest during a year.

ᛋ **Sól:** Known as the runic symbol for the sun and the goddess Sol in Germanic mythology. It also represents success and wholeness.

ᛏ **Týr:** The runic symbol of the god Tyr, also associated with victory, honor, and power.

ᛒ **Björk or Bjarkan:** Translated as "birch," this rune symbolizes the birch tree. It's also linked to the superior goddess, new life, and birth.

ᛘ **Maðr:** Known as "man" in modern English, this rune represents the first man - Mannus. It's also associated with family, planning, awareness, intelligence, and continuity.

ᛚ **Lögr:** Translated as "sea," it's the symbol of the vital life force and feminine energy.

ᛦ **Yr:** Known as "yew" in modern English, this rune symbolizes death, the underworld, and the journey between the two worlds.

Rune Casting Techniques

Before delving into the different rune-casting techniques, you should consider finding a quiet space for your practice. When you've found your quiet spot and are ready to start, sit comfortably and focus your mind. You can do this through deep breathing, meditation, or any other relaxing exercise.

Think about what question or questions you want to ask. You can also say a prayer or call upon your spiritual guide at this point. Place a rune cloth on your altar or table. You'll lay runes on this.

There are many ways to cast runes, and you can select the one that suits you the best. Your choice should always reflect your experience and the type of information you're seeking about the future. Some techniques offer in-depth knowledge about future events, while others are ideal for quick confirmation. Learn the significance of each rune before you start attempting either spread. This also helps you become more confident in relying on your gut feeling. You can do this by simply picking up the runes one by one, reading up on their meaning, and contemplating how they resonate with you. Once you have this information, you'll be ready to do the layouts below.

The Three Rune Layout

If you are a rune-casting novice, this layout is the easiest to understand and will help you to move on to other types of casting. However, even experienced practitioners can use it to consult on simple matters. It's recommended to ask only one or two questions. Here is how to cast it:

With your question in mind, select three runes from the bag and put them on the cloth.

You'll be reading them from left to right.

Rune number 1 indicates your overall situation related to the question.

Rune number 2 shows a possible challenge or issue related to the question.

Rune number 3 represents the best course of action to overcome the challenge.

The Five Rune Layout

Once you've practiced divination with the first technique and learned to rely more on your intuition, you can try out the 5-rune layout. It gives you a little more insight than the previous one. Here is how to read it:

Form the question in your mind (about what is to come) and blindly choose 5 runes from the bag.

Place the first rune in the center of your divination area.

The next rune goes to the left, then one above, one below, and the final one to the right. You should have a cross shape.

You can place all the runes face up or face down. It does not matter as long as you turn them all face up at some point.

The horizontal line composed of three runes will show your timeline – what has come, what is now, and what will come.

The rune to the left indicates possible issues you need to accept and overcome.

The rune to the right shows how you can access help to overcome the issue.

The 7-Rune Layout

The 7-rune layout is another cast you can use to further develop your intuition. It also gives a little more insight into the subject you're interested in. Here is how to read the 7-rune cast:

Focusing on your intention, take seven runes out of the bag, and lay them out in a V shape.

Start reading from the top left portion of the V, go down, and then up again.

The rune at the top left of the V shows what once was.

The next rune gives you your present circumstances.

The next will show you what is still to come.

The rune at the bottom point of the V indicates actions to take to move you forward in your life.

The next rune on the upward turn shows your current emotions.

The rune two spots away from the bottom point shows your issues.

The last rune gives the possibilities for your future.

The 9-Rune Cast

9 is a sacred number in many numerologies, and casting in nines amplifies the power of the runes. It's great for exploring your position in your spiritual path and the opportunities that lay ahead of you. This cast is recommended for medium-to-difficult-level practitioners who have developed a higher level of intuition. Here is how to do it:

Consider your spiritual journey and what desires you want to fulfill while on it.

Take nine runes out of their bag and hold them in your hands.

Toss the runes out on a cloth and look at them.

The runes closer to the center of the cloth will be the most relevant to your question.

Also, pay attention to runes touching each other - as these may denote complementary influences. Runes on the opposite side of the cloth are opposing forces.

Start interpreting the runes that have their engravings face up. You can even write the message down and revisit it later.

Then, turn the ones facing down and read them as well. They often indicated outcomes you haven't considered before.

Contemplate the meaning of all runes while tapping into your intuition.

The 24-Rune Layout

This cast is usually used for annual divination practices, as it allows the querent to get an insight into what they might expect in the coming year. Here is how to read the 24-rune layout:

Spread out the runes by forming a 3x8 grid. You'll start reading from the first row, from right to left.

The first rune shows the ways you could achieve prosperity.

The second rune shows the ways to become healthier and stronger.

The third rune shows ways to defend yourself.

The fourth rune shows ways to gain wisdom, inspiration, and motivation.

The fifth rune shows the direction your life's path will most likely take during the year.

The sixth rune shows all the wisdom you can learn during the year.

The seventh rune shows all the skills you can achieve and the gifts you can have.

The eighth rune of the first row shows the ways you can achieve happiness.

The first rune of the second row (read from right to left) symbolizes changes.

The second rune denotes what you need to obtain your goals.

The third rune represents the obstacles you face when working towards your goals.

The fourth rune symbolizes all the achievements you can reach during the year.

The fifth rune illustrates the choices you'll need to make.

The sixth rune symbolizes the ways your inner skills will manifest.

The seventh rune denotes pivotal life situations you'll find yourself in.

The eighth rune of the second row symbolizes the energy guiding you on your path.

The first rune of the third row represents all your business and legal affairs.

The second rune represents the way you'll achieve growth in different areas of life.

The third rune represents friendships and family relationships.

The fourth rune represents your social status.

The fifth rune represents your emotions.

The sixth rune represents romantic and sexual relationships.

The seventh rune represents the ways you'll obtain a balance between different areas of life.

The eighth rune represents all the assets you'll gain during the year.

Chapter 10: Crystal Divination

The art of divination is so vast that you can spend your entire life learning the various parts of predicting the future. Practicing divination helps you connect with the divine and allows you to seek guidance from them regarding matters of your life. The insights gained by following these practices often originate from one's consciousness but require the use of divinatory tools to access them.

Crystals play an important role as one of the tools for divination.
https://unsplash.com/photos/p0XN3fz6J2c

Crystal divination is one of the tools used to access divine guidance and wisdom. Crystals have always played an essential role in many divinatory techniques, be it in the early ages or during modern times. Several techniques in crystal divination can be employed depending on what kind of wisdom you seek. You can either use a single technique and get your answer or choose multiple crystal divinity techniques to gain insight. Moreover, the crystals you select also depend on the type of divination technique you'd use. However, you do not need to spend a fortune on rare crystals for any technique. In fact, a proper crystal selection process should be followed when practicing particular divination techniques.

While crystal divination is not as complicated as other divination techniques, there are still a few details you should keep in mind when practicing it. So, this chapter will provide a detailed guide about the various methods of crystal divination, mainly lithomancy and crystallomancy. It also provides a list of crystals and gemstones that can be used in these processes and their interpretations.

Common Crystals Used for Divination

Crystal magic has been practiced for centuries, and while divination practices don't exactly classify as magic, there is some special power within crystals that makes them so valuable for these practices. Each type of crystal or gemstone has a unique property and symbolizes different things. Each of these crystals is also said to have specific energies or frequencies that make them unique. Crystals are used in various rituals, healing spells, and protection techniques. You can tap into the unique energies of these crystals and use them to get predictions and wisdom. To understand and interpret crystal divination readings, you need to learn what each crystal symbolizes.

Aquamarine - If you're waiting for the ideal time or opportunity, don't. Make a move right now.

Carnelian - Seek the proper balance in your life, and don't settle with whatever life gives you. Alloy happiness, love, and color into your life.

Heliotrope - Do not act impulsively. You need to learn how to persevere through this. Remain completely focused on your goals and stand your ground to achieve them.

Hematite - Don't succumb to societal pressure or what others expect of you. Don't ignore your wants and needs just for the sake of other people.

Lapis Lazuli - Pace yourself, slow down, and think through before making any decisions or acting rashly. You'll see your efforts being noticed.

Amber - Beware of what you're giving up and consider if you're getting anything from the transaction. Know what you truly want and make a decision based on that.

Clear Quartz - New information will be revealed, which will bring you clarity. Simply stay focused on your goals, retain your honesty, and you'll soon have a fresh perspective.

Malachite - Move on from what you are holding onto and concentrate on what you want and need.

Citrine - Communicate your thoughts with honesty and integrity, and you'll have a positive response. Peace and prosperity are in your future.

Amazonite - You need to take a strong stance on your beliefs now that your life is changing. Right now is the time for a fresh start and new adventures.

Moonstone - Don't be scared to speak the truth and convey your real feelings. Just go with the flow and try not to force or block anything.

Rose Quartz - It's time to forgive yourself for past mistakes and learn not to take the blame for others' mistakes as your own. Find support from those around you.

Pyrite - Be observant of any changes in attitude or deception that might take place. There is more than what can only be seen, and you should look deeper.

Labradorite - You might need a change of circumstances to achieve your goals, but be careful what you wish for, as it might not be good for you.

Blue Lace Agate - You'll need to communicate about the issue soon, and it is essential that you open up and share your true feelings.

Tiger's Eye - You should expect good news, new beginnings, and successes. However, you'll need focus and confidence to achieve this.

Unakite - You may be feeling uncertain, but going backward won't help and will only cause your problems to repeat themselves.

Tree Agate - Get to the root of your issues, and begin strengthening your roots. You'll find answers there.

Snowflake Obsidian - You're soon going to gain clarity about a situation, but you'll need to make the right choice.

Rutilated Quartz - You'll see everything coming together soon, but don't hesitate to reach out to your loved ones for help.

Depending on the crystal divination technique you follow, you'll need to choose single or multiple crystals. Once you've chosen the crystals and gemstones of your choice, you'll need to cleanse their energies before using them in a ritual. Once they're cleansed, they will need to be infused with your intention for the process.

Crystal Divination or Lithomancy

Lithomancy is a fortune-telling approach involving throwing crystals and interpreting information based on where they land. It's a pretty complicated technique and requires complete focus to master it. However, once you master it, you'll be making expert readings in no time. Although the use of stones is common practice for lithomancy techniques, crystal divinity techniques use crystals and gemstones for readings. Lithomancy can be dated back over 5,000 years, and evidence has been found for it in Persia. Most things change over time, and Lithomancy is no different – it has been adapted by many cultures, including the Romans, Egyptians, and Greeks. Today, the technique is still used by a large number of people to get insight into their future. The process of lithomancy involves the following steps:

Choose the Stones

To start with the lithomancy ritual, you'll first have to get together a crystal set of all the essential gemstones and crystals. To choose the ones suitable for you, refer to the crystal property tables at the end of this chapter. Once you have your set, you'll start to become familiar with them. It's best to use a combination of 13 crystals at a time and then replace them with every session. Pick out the crystals that resonate most with you, or embody the characteristics you're looking for.

Create a Casting Area

Once you've collected the casting stones, it's time to create the casting area where the technique will be performed. Be careful of your casting area – you'll prepare it physically, but you must also prepare it spiritually. If you carry around a lot of negative energy, you'll be stunted in your casting. Mark the area of casting by placing ropes around the area, laying out a cloth, or pouring salt to mark the boundaries.

If you are using cloth to mark your casting area, the most common cloth is black silk – more than being just a demarcation of boundaries, black silk is an object of ritual within Lithomancy. Failing that, you can mark the casting area with Himalayan salt. Do this by spreading a fine trickle of salt to form a circle the size of a basket. You'll need to cleanse the casting space by using smoke to remove any negative energies within the space.

Cast the Stones

Casting the crystals will be the major part of this divination process and will ultimately decide what readings you get. You'll need to empty your mind of any negative thoughts and feelings and put your complete focus on the task at hand. For this process, you'll need the following:

Gemstones or crystals

A silk cloth or mat

A bowl of water

First, you need to clean the gemstones and remove any negative energies they might have picked up. Do this by dipping the crystals in the bowl of water and imagining all the negative energies leaving the crystal. Carefully take the crystals out of the water and dry them off with a spare cloth.

Next, gather the casting stones between the palms of your hands, and position your hands about two to three inches above the casting area. Shut your eyes and take a deep breath in and out, in and out. Clear out your head, and remove every thought that's on your mind. Once your mind is blank and you feel calm, bring your hand close to your heart, and focus on the question at hand. Ask the universe or guides to help answer your question. Finally, drop the stones onto the surface while keeping your eyes closed.

Once you open your eyes, you'll see a pattern formed by the crystals. Any gems that have fallen outside the casting space should be considered irrelevant to your question. The crystals inside the casting space will convey what the universe is trying to tell you. The crystal closest to the center of the space will be the main indicator to answer your question. Other crystals will represent any other advice you should take into consideration. However, if no stones fall into the casting area, you'll have to repeat the process and possibly rephrase your question.

Interpret the Results

The final step of the process will be to interpret the results of your reading. This is also a crucial step requiring deep concentration and a good understanding of the meanings of each gemstone. Your casting area has different sections, and each one signifies the relevance of the crystals that fall into it. For instance, if the crystal is dropped into the inner side of the casting circle, it will significantly impact your overall reading.

Whereas the gem that lies on the outermost section of the casting space will be of little importance. To make an interpretation, you'll need to connect the meanings and representations that each gemstone is associated with and connect them with their level of significance based on where they land. So, you'll end up with a clear and precise answer to your question/s.

As a lithomancy practitioner, keeping a journal tracking every reading is good practice. This will help you interpret your readings faster and make it easy for future interpretations. So, whether you're interpreting your own reading or someone else's, make sure to track the various interpretations. Other ways to interpret the casting stones include:

Once you've cast the stones, remove the crystals that have fallen out of the casting boundary and close your eyes once again. Focus on your question again and pick a stone from the casting space. This is the stone that answers your question.

Another method is the triple stone method, where you have to pick three casting stones from the casting space, one by one. The stones represent the past, present, and future.

Alternatively, Use a Lithomancy Chart

Once you've had enough practice with the basic stone casting techniques, you can move on to more complicated processes, including a lithomancy chart. Using one will give a much more detailed interpretation of your readings. To use a lithomancy chart while casting stones, replace the casting mat or silk cloth with the lithomancy chart.

There are a few ways to design a lithomancy chart, the most common being a combination of three wheels, each divided into twelve sections. The wheels are directly related to the astrological signs relevant to your life: physical, emotional, spiritual, and more. When you cast the stones, you'll then be able to read them based on what each one denotes. For instance, if the aquamarine crystal lands on the career section of the chart, and you're currently struggling to decide whether or not to change jobs, this would be your sign to make a move for it.

Another method to make a lithomancy chart is to make the exact same number of sections as your crystals. Then, close your eyes and place a crystal on each section instead of throwing them randomly. This will provide you with insight into every aspect of your life, contrasting with the casting method, where multiple crystals could land on a single section. However, some people prefer the throwing method because sometimes you might need insight into one aspect of your life more than the others.

Once you're done with the casting process and interpreting the readings, the next step is to act on the insights you've gleaned. For instance, if you've obtained a negative reading, you need to take the necessary precautions and advice that were foretold to avoid any bad luck coming your way. On the other hand, if you get a positive reading, you can sit back and relax.

The best course of action after reading is to plan for the future accordingly because our choices in the present have a huge impact on how our future is shaped. Remember that the art of lithomancy is simply a tool to help you figure out the course of action. However, it is not set in stone, and the final decision is always up to you.

Crystal Ball Reading or Crystallomancy

Crystallomancy or crystal ball reading is another method of crystal divination that is popular to see into the future. The technique uses crystals shaped into spheres to make predictions about the future. Although you can use any kind of crystal, the most commonly used one for this method is clear quartz. Crystal ball reading might come naturally to a select few, but most have to work at the process.

Crystallomancy (crystal ball reading) first requires you to form a bond with the crystal. This means proper care of your crystal ball and not only a spiritual bond. Be sure to keep the ball clean and overlay it with a silk cloth when it is not in use. When using the ball, treat it respectfully, and store it well. This way, its energy will remain pure and personal to you. It is best to use the crystal ball when your head is free from negative thoughts and you have a complete focus on the task.

To begin scrying, follow these simple steps:

Take a light source (Candle, lamp, or torch) and place it to the side of the crystal ball. This is done to ensure that the light does not interfere with the image being formed in the crystal. Turn off all other lights in the room.

Close your eyes and bring the intended question to your mind. Take three deep breaths before opening your eyes.

Stare into the crystal until your gaze starts to drift, and you have the feeling of being both awake and not awake. Do not focus on the ball, but keep your gaze on it. After a while, some images will start to appear in the ball.

These images will not necessarily be clear and might not even make sense at the moment. Plus, most of these images will be symbolic in nature and will only make sense when you relate them to your current circumstances.

Once you've clearly understood what you observed in the crystal ball, note it down in your scrying journal. You could also simply scribble the vision down onto the journal and try to make sense of it later.

Crystal Cleansing Tips

Before you can practice any divination techniques with your crystals, you must cleanse them of any negative energies they might have picked up. This ensures that they work in harmony with your intentions and that the process goes smoothly. Some ways to cleanse your crystals include:

Take a bowl of clean water and add Himalayan pink salt or sea salt to the bowl. Stir the mixture until the salt dissolves, and then slowly dip the crystals into the water. Allow the crystals to soak for a little bit before taking them out and drying them off.

Another method is to place the crystals directly in the sun. The sunlight is said to clear away any negative energies and will recharge the crystals with pure energy.

Crystal divination is a fascinating way to get insights into the future. It has been around for centuries and has gained popularity over time. The process usually gives good results and accurate descriptions of the future. However, you should remember that it is simply a tool to help figure out the best plan of action for your future and does not actually determine what it is.

Bonus: Glossary of Terms

This last chapter contains some of the terminology most often used across the different divination methods mentioned in the book. You can use it as a reference whenever you feel the need to revisit information about a specific term.

Air Hands: Bony hands with protruding knuckles belonging to curious and analytical people with good communication skills.

Air Signs: Gemini, Libra, and Aquarius.

Altar: A sacred place where divinations and other acts of magic are performed.

Angles: Ascendant: the first cusp, Innum Coeli: the cusp of the fourth, Descendant: the cusp of the seventh, and Midheaven: the tenth cusp. All houses of the zodiac.

Ascendant: The rising sign that is apparent at the time of a person's birth on the eastern horizon.

Aspects: The relationships the planets make with each other when traveling in their orbits around the sun.

Astrology: The science of determining future events and experiences based on the position of celestial bodies at the time and place of one's birth.

Aura: The field of electromagnetic energy surrounding a person's body.

Binding: Restricting, focusing, or combining energies of several magical objects and tools.

Blueprint: An overall makeup of one's personality, reflected in their name, the numbers associated with their life, and life path.

Cardinal Signs: The signs associated with season changes:- Aries (winter-spring), Cancer (spring-summer), Libra (summer-autumn), and Capricorn (autumn-winter).

Chakras: Major energy points in the body through which the vital life force can be accessed and manipulated.

Circle: A sacred space created for the protection of the diviner during their practice.

Challenge Numbers: Numbers represent events, circumstances, and situations designed to help you prepare for large and challenging opportunities in life.

Channel: Communicating messages between different sources, worlds, and spiritual planes.

Charm: An object enriched with magical properties like protection, added strength, etc.

Clairsentience: The ability to use multiple senses to receive messages during divinatory and other practices.

Clairvoyance: The ability to clearly visualize images related to past, present, or future events.

Cornerstone: A person's strongest trait, approach to finances, or essence of their name, represented by the first letter in their first name.

Crystal Ball: An object made of crystals with magical properties, which allows you to predict future events.

Cusp: The margins of the zone represented by a zodiac house and the degree beginning at one sign and ending at another.

Descendant: Sitting opposite the ascendant is the cusp of the zodiac's seventh house.

Divinistic Dream Interpretation: Predicting the future by interpreting answers you get in your dreams after consulting Tarot cards and other divination tools.

Earth Hands: Firm and fleshy hands belonging to grounded, logical, and practical **persons.**

Earth Signs: Virgo, Capricorn, and Taurus.

Elder Futhark: An alphabet denoted by symbols that was developed by the people who inhabited Scandinavia, parts of Britain, and some smaller regions of Europe.

Electional Astrology: A branch of astrology that involves choosing preferred times for important events.

Elements: Water, Fire, Air, and Earth – each related to three zodiac signs.

Empath: A person drawn to other people's feelings and aligns their own according to what they pick up from others.

Emphatic Aspects: Aspects that align the energies of two planets with one another, like Conjunction or Opposition.

Fate Line: The line running up and down your palm that tells you what the future has in store.

Feminine Signs: Feminine signs are more receptive to negative energy – Pisces, Virgo, Scorpio, Taurus, Cancer, and Capricorn.

Fire Hands: Hands with distinctive creases and mounds - belonging to individuals with a confident, industrious and passionate nature.

Fire Signs: Leo, Aries, and Sagittarius.

Fixed Signs: Taurus, Leo, Scorpio, and Aquarius.

Frequency: The levels of energy projected towards people, objects, and situations in your environment.

Glyphs: Symbols denoting planets, astrological signs, luminary bodies, aspects, and constellations.

Grounding: Rooting yourself to the physical world to increase focus during divination or other magical acts.

Guide: An entity that provides guidance for personal growth and awareness.

Head Line: The line in the center of your palm - represents intellectual curiosity and personal goals.

Heart Line: The line above the headline - is associated with relationships, emotions, and other matters of the heart.

Holistic: Natural healing methods encompassing techniques to cure ailments of mind, body, and soul.

Houses: The 12 zones of the elliptical space across the sky, ruling over specific areas of life depending on the time of birth.

Inner Mars: Located above the thumb, this is the part of the hand representing aggression.

Insight: Using intuition to access and analyze information relevant to the question.

Intuition: Also called protective sight, it is the ability to raise yourself to an elevated state of psychic awareness.

Invocation: Calling upon a guide for assistance to decipher psychic messages.

Karma: The sum of past actions with negative consequences to your current life.

Karmic Debt: The four numbers (13, 14, 16, 19) represent the debt given to souls who must face karma to correct their past mistakes.

Karmic Lessons: Lessons every soul learns during each life cycle.

Life Line: Is found below the head lid on the palm and deals with major events in life: experiences, health, values, and morals.

Lifepath: Also called the destiny number, determines a person's intellect and important lessons to learn before moving on to the next life cycle.

Luminary Objects: the Sun and the Moon.

Major Arcana: A set of 22 cards denoting the pivotal aspects of one's life, including relationships, family, career, health, and more.

Masculine Signs: Masculine signs are more receptive to positive energy. They are Aquarius, Leo, Libra, Gemini, Aries, and Sagittarius.

Master Number: Double-digit numbers like 11, 22, and 33 in one's blueprint can boost their strength and noble personality traits.

Meditation: The practice of relaxation, which results in increased focus during divinatory and other practices.

Minor c: The deck of 56 cards representing smaller or temporary influences in one's life.

Mounts: Areas of flesh on the palm that can denote areas of your life. They relate to the major planets in our solar system.

Mutable Signs: Virgo, Gemini, Sagittarius, and Pisces.

Natal Chart: Also known as a birth chart, the natal chart reveals a person's traits and possible future according to the placement of the planets at the time of their birth.

Numerology: The art of predicting one's past, present, and future based on the most important numbers in their life.

Odin: The Norse god of wisdom, magic, poetry, death, and divination, who brought the runes to the people.

Orb: The range or distance within which a planet can influence another planet.

Outer Mars: Out with Inner Mars – deals with courage, emotion, and perseverance.

Palmistry: Also called chiromancy, palmistry is the practice of predicting one's future path by looking at the lines on their palm.

Part of Fortune: The section of the natal chart denoting an aspect in which a person has a natural aptitude.

Personal Planets: Planets with a direct effect on one's personality.

Personal Year: The number determined by one's personal blueprint. It allows insight into potential events and experiences in one's future.

Pinnacle: Unique opportunities are presented at each life cycle based on a person's blueprint numbers.

Plain of Mars: The area in the center of the palm that creates an equilibrium between the Outer and Inner Mars.

Precognition: The ability to foresee future events, situations, and circumstances.

Prediction: Messages indicating future outcomes or events.

Prophecy: Prediction made by someone with a heightened ability to reveal the future.

Reading: Accessing information (through intuition and psychic abilities) that may answer the question presented by the reader.

Regression: The ability to access information relevant to the future from the past.

Runes: Symbols with magical properties – used for divination, protection, and other magical purposes.

Rune Casting: The practice of interpreting the meaning of runes for divinatory purposes.

Runic Alphabet: Also known as futhark, an ancient alphabet consisting of runes instead of letters.

Quadrants: Groups of houses, beginning with the first, fourth, seventh, and tenth zodiac houses.

Querent: The person who presents the question about the future.

Retrograde: Apparent backward motion of a planet in relation to the Earth, resulting in the planet's negative influences on people's lives.

Scrying: Using a crystal ball (or another reflective material) to look into the future.

Speculum: A magical object used for scrying.

Sun Line: The line from the base of the hand to the pinky finger that symbolizes fame and fortune, how we are perceived in public, and what we will leave behind.

Sun sign: A person's sun sign denotes the house in which the sun resided during the time of their birth.

Synastry: A specific sublet of relationship astrology.

Tarot: A deck of 78 cards used to predict future events.

Tarot Reading: Interpreting the meaning of individual tarot cards or tarot spreads.

Waning Moon: The phase between the full moon and the new moon.

Water Hands: Hands are soft to the touch, denoting awareness of emotions, psychic abilities, and intuition.

Water Signs: Scorpio, Pisces, and Cancer.

Waxing moon: The phase between the new moon and the full moon.

Well of Fate: The source of all wisdom, including the one contained in the ancient runes.

Wheel of the Year: One cycle of the seasonal year, consisting of eight seasons.

Younger Futhark: A simplified version of the original runic alphabet developed during the Viking Age.

Zodiac: A circle divided into 12 equal sectors of 30 degrees represented by the zodiac signs and houses.

Conclusion

Divination is an ancient art that has been used for centuries for various purposes. It can be used in magic or just as a guide for spiritual growth. One of the oldest divination methods is astrology – the art of discerning the future by looking at the sky. Astrology associates earthly events with the positions and movements of celestial bodies, including the sun, the moon, the planets, and stellar constellations. These bodies are linked to the 12 zodiac houses, which are shown by the Earth's 24-hour trip around its orbit, and the 12 zodiac signs, which are shown by the sun's path around the Earth every year.

Numerology is another well-known method, which is the art of working out a person's life path from their numbers. Apart from carrying a magical meaning, numbers also have planetary correspondences. Adding together the numbers that make up your date of birth – year, month, and day – you can better decipher the secrets hidden within you. This is similar to looking at the positions and movements of the planets.

The most commonly used divination method is tarot. However, contrary to popular belief, tarot cards won't help you predict the future. They only offer a general guideline for future outcomes. How you interpret them is up to you - and the forces affecting your work. The secret to its popularity is twofold. You can use it to increase self-awareness and reflect on your values and life, answer someone else's questions, or simply for developing your intuition. Another benefit of tarot is that there are numerous spreads you can choose from.

Palmistry, or chiromancy, is another divination technique practiced by several ancient civilizations. In palmistry, you're looking into someone's hand to explore their personality traits to determine how their characteristics, thoughts, emotions, and actions may affect their future. Each hand is associated with different brain activities, and each line on one's hand is an expression of these activities. Since most activities are the result of your core personality, interpreting them can give you an insight into how your future may unfold.

Runes are symbols of different magical properties. Traditionally, runes are engraved on wood or stone - although they can also be written on a piece of paper or painted on a talisman to be carried with you. Engraved runes are carried in a protective bag. When needed, they are tossed out, and questions asked, generally about future events. As in the case of tarot cards, the runes facing up carry the most likely answers. Written runes are typically used for protection, reflection, or drawing in positive forces.

Similar to runes, crystals also have magical properties. They can soak in both positive and negative energy. Lithomancy, or divination with crystals and stones, is also a more accurate method to discern the future. Crystals can be used alone or in a grid, harnessing their cumulative powers. Crystal ball divination is a specific form of divinatory method. It involves gazing into a crystal ball, asking questions about the future, and interpreting the answers based on the images shown in the ball. It requires deep focus and the ability to eliminate any unrelated thoughts from one's mind to avoid misinterpretation of the messages.

Here's another book by Silvia Hill that you might like

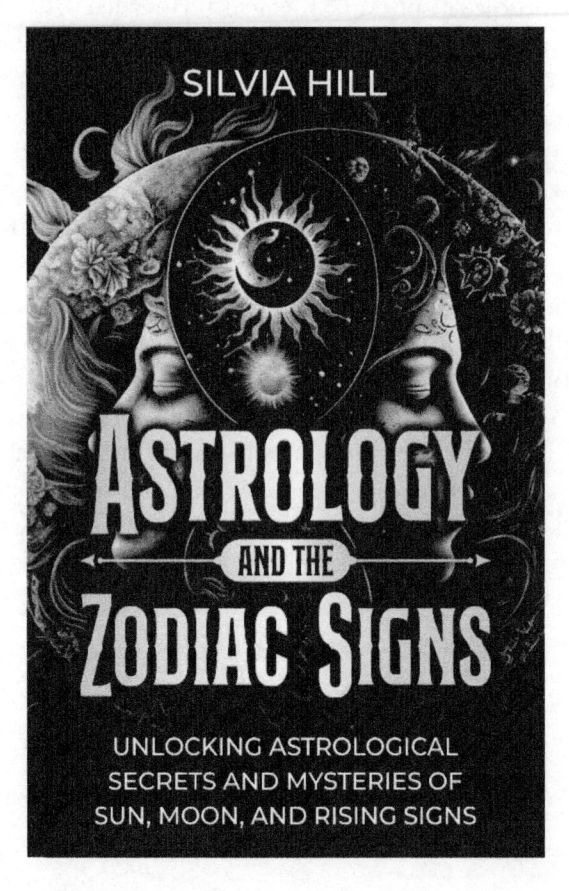

Free Bonus from Silvia Hill available for limited time

Hi Spirituality Lovers!

My name is Silvia Hill, and first off, I want to THANK YOU for reading my book.

Now you have a chance to join my exclusive spirituality email list so you can get the ebooks below for free as well as the potential to get more spirituality ebooks for free! Simply click the link below to join.

P.S. Remember that it's 100% free to join the list.

~~$27~~ FREE BONUSES

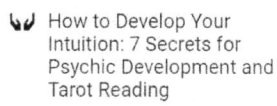

- 9 Types of Spirit Guides and How to Connect to Them
- How to Develop Your Intuition: 7 Secrets for Psychic Development and Tarot Reading
- Tarot Reading Secrets for Love, Career, and General Messages

Access your free bonuses here
https://livetolearn.lpages.co/pendulum-and-divination-paperback/

References

Desy, P. L. (n.d.). What is Dowsing? Learn Religions. https://www.learnreligions.com/what-is-dowsing-1731451

Oakes, J. (2021, September 21). How To Use A Pendulum: The A-Z Guide. Tiny Rituals. https://tinyrituals.co/blogs/tiny-rituals/how-to-use-a-pendulum

Webster, R. (2002). Pendulum magic for beginners: Power to achieve all goals. Llewellyn Publications.

Pendulum users from the past. (n.d.). Google.Com. https://sites.google.com/site/westmorlanddowsers/pendulum-users-from-the-past

Tucker, C. (2020, September 7). The History of a Pendulum. Wilde Folk. https://shopwildefolk.com/blogs/news/the-history-of-a-pendulum

Pendulum Dowsing – An Introduction to Using a Pendulum. (n.d.). Holistic Shop. https://www.holisticshop.co.uk/articles/guide-pendulum-dowsing

Barbara. (2015, May 8). Wooden pendulum. Colorful Crafts; Barbara. https://colorful-crafts.com/wooden-pendulum/

Choosing crystals. (n.d.). Thecrystalhealer.co.uk. http://www.thecrystalhealer.co.uk/Crystal-Information/Choosing-Crystals

Mike. (2015, August 17). Different pendulums and their uses. Instant Karma Asheville. https://www.instantkarmaasheville.com/different-pendulums-and-their-uses/

Wigington, P. (2009, March 17). Learn to use a pendulum for divination. Learn Religions. https://www.learnreligions.com/pendulum-divination-2561760

Abundance Mindset Mama. (2021, July 1). How to cleanse A pendulum-5 easy ways. Abundance Mindset Mama. https://abundancemindsetmama.com/how-to-cleanse-a-pendulum

Huberman, L. (2020, September 6). How to charge + cleanse a pendulum. Ark Made. https://ark-made.com/blogs/guides/how-to-charge-cleanse-a-pendulum

Julia. (2017, June 24). Pendulums 101: how to cleanse, program, and care for your pendulum. Julia North. https://julianorth.co/blog/2017/06/pendulums-101-cleansing-programming-and-caring-for-your-pendulum

p-themes. (n.d.). Cleansing & charging. Cinnabar Soul. https://cinnabarsoul.com/collections/cleansing-charging/pendulum

Samantha. (2020, February 28). How to cleanse A pendulum: 5 strong & easy ways. Tea & Rosemary. https://teaandrosemary.com/cleanse-pendulum/

Ask Your Pendulum. (n.d.). How to use a pendulum. Ask Your Pendulum. https://askyourpendulum.com/pages/how-to-use-a-pendulum

Cleansing, charging, and programming your pendulum. (n.d.). The Angel's Medium. https://www.theangelsmedium.com/programming-your-pendulum

Creating your own Sacred Space in your Home. (n.d.). NATALIA KUNA | Intuitive, Healer | Creator of Spiritual Course Academy. https://www.nataliakuna.com/creating-your-own-sacred-space.html

How to program your pendulum. (2019, May 16). FreerSpirit Akashic Soul Readings. https://freerspirit.com/2019/05/16/how-to-program-your-pendulum/

Voss, S. (2019, July 3). Creating a Sacred Space using Crystal Energy. Earth Family Crystals. https://earthfamilycrystals.com/blogs/default-blog/creating-a-sacred-space-using-crystal-energy

A beginner's guide to 10 types of crystals & how to use each of them. (2021, May 12). Mindbodygreen. https://www.mindbodygreen.com/articles/types-of-crystals

Ashley. (2021, November 18). 6 of the best crystal pendulums to have. Moon of Gemini. https://moonofgemini.com/crystal-pendulums/

Caroline, E. (2021, May 17). Crystals for chakra healing. Ohana; Ohana Yoga + Barre. https://ohanayoga.com/crystals-for-chakra-healing/

CASTLE MARKETING. (2019, October 4). Grounding with crystals. Crystal Castle. https://www.crystalcastle.com.au/grounding-with-crystals/

Estrada, J. (2021, February 16). 10 types of crystals for healing, self-love, energy clearing, and positivity. Well+Good. https://www.wellandgood.com/types-crystals/

Keithley, Z. (2022, June 15). 7 grounding crystals and stones for stability & protection. Zanna Keithley. https://zannakeithley.com/grounding-crystals-and-stones/

Lindberg, S. (2020, August 24). What are chakras? Meaning, location, and how to unblock them. Healthline. https://www.healthline.com/health/what-are-chakras

Mike. (2015, August 17). Different pendulums and their uses. Instant Karma Asheville. https://www.instantkarmaasheville.com/different-pendulums-and-their-uses/

Owen, N. (2020, April 21). Healing crystals guide: the best crystals for you and how to use them. Cosmopolitan. https://www.cosmopolitan.com/uk/worklife/a32144127/healing-crystals/

Palermo, E., & Gordon, J. (2022, January 25). Crystal healing: Stone-cold facts about gemstone treatments. Livescience.com; Live Science. https://www.livescience.com/40347-crystal-healing.html

Rekstis, E. (2022, January 21). Everything you need to know about healing crystals and their benefits. Healthline. https://www.healthline.com/health/mental-health/guide-to-healing-crystals

Roots, A. (n.d.). Seven Chakra Pendulum. Angelic Roots. https://www.angelicroots.com/products/seven-chakra-pendulum

Scoop, S. (2022, June 1). 25 best crystals to use for grounding and healing energy. Sarah Scoop. https://sarahscoop.com/25-best-crystals-to-use-for-grounding-and-healing-energy/

Sylvester, M. (2022, June 30). These are the best crystals for each chakra. Nylon. https://www.nylon.com/life/crystals-for-each-chakra

The science behind healing crystals explained! (2019, August 1). The Times of India; Times Of India. https://timesofindia.indiatimes.com/life-style/health-fitness/home-remedies/the-science-behind-healing-crystals-explained/articleshow/70482968.cms

Veronese, L. (2022, June 23). A complete guide to the best crystals for each chakra. Hello Glow. https://helloglow.co/crystals-for-chakras/

Walters, M. (2021, September 17). Are healing crystals for real? Here's what the science says. Healthline. https://www.healthline.com/health/healing-crystals-what-they-can-do-and-what-they-cant

We Thieves, C. (2019, September 9). An introduction to crystals and their healing properties. We Thieves.

What are chakras? (n.d.). WebMD. https://www.webmd.com/balance/what-are-chakras

Zoldan, R. J. (2020, June 22). Your 7 chakras, explained—plus, how to tell if they're blocked. Well+Good. https://www.wellandgood.com/what-are-chakras/

Pendulum Dowsing – An Introduction to Using a Pendulum. (n.d.). Holistic Shop. https://www.holisticshop.co.uk/articles/guide-pendulum-dowsing

Davis, F. (2021, July 22). Dowsing With a Pendulum: What It Is, How It Works & How To Do It. Cosmic Cuts. https://cosmiccuts.com/blogs/healing-stones-blog/dowsing-with-a-pendulum

Aletheia. (2017, December 18). How to Use a Dowsing Pendulum For Divination - Beginner's Guide ★. LonerWolf. https://lonerwolf.com/dowsing-pendulum/

Store, E. M. W. (2021, April 24). How to Use a Pendulum for Divination. East Meets West USA. https://www.eastmeetswestusa.com/blogs/east-meets-west-blog-articles/how-to-use-a-pendulum-for-divination

Davis, F. (2021, July 22). Dowsing With a Pendulum: What It Is, How It Works & How To Do It. Cosmic Cuts. https://cosmiccuts.com/blogs/healing-stones-blog/dowsing-with-a-pendulum

Kinsey, E. (n.d.). What is divination: a beginners guide. Spirit and Destiny. https://www.spiritanddestiny.co.uk/wellbeing-and-mindfulness/spirituality/what-is-divination/

Kinsey, E. (n.d.). What is a pendulum and how to use it for guidance or spiritual healing. Spirit and Destiny. https://www.spiritanddestiny.co.uk/wellbeing-and-mindfulness/spirituality/what-is-a-pendulum/

Ask Your Pendulum. (n.d.-a). How to use pendulum charts. Ask Your Pendulum. https://askyourpendulum.com/pages/how-to-use-pendulum-charts

Ask Your Pendulum. (n.d.-b). How to use your pendulum with a multiple choice chart. Ask Your Pendulum. https://askyourpendulum.com/pages/how-to-use-your-pendulum-with-a-multiple-choice-chart

Paige, A. (2009, April 9). How to make a pendulum chart. Synonym.com; Synonym. https://classroom.synonym.com/how-to-make-a-pendulum-chart-12078741.html

Pendulum dowsing manual guide + free sample pendulum charts. (n.d.). Abundance Belief. https://abundancebelief.com/product/pendulum-dowsing-manual-free-sample-charts/

Use a pendulum chart * Wicca-spirituality.com. (n.d.). Wicca-spirituality.com https://www.wicca-spirituality.com/pendulum-chart.html

A beginner's guide to the 7 chakras. (2009, October 28). Mindbodygreen. https://www.mindbodygreen.com/articles/7-chakras-for-beginners

Ask Your Pendulum. (n.d.). How to use your pendulum to check the status of your chakras. Ask Your Pendulum. https://askyourpendulum.com/pages/how-to-use-your-pendulum-to-check-the-status-of-your-chakras

Energy Work With Pendulums, Crystals, and Reiki (2013) - Lynn Marie Gravatt. (n.d.). Scribd. https://www.scribd.com/document/346157723/energy-work-with-pendulums-crystals-and-reiki-2013-lynn-marie-gravatt

How to balance your chakras with a pendulum. (n.d.). Gaia. https://www.gaia.com/article/how-balance-your-chakras-pendulum

Hughes, L. (2019, March 1). What are healing crystals and do they actually work? Oprah Daily. https://www.oprahdaily.com/life/health/a26559820/healing-crystals/

Shah, P. (2020, August 20). A primer of the chakra system. Chopra. https://chopra.com/articles/what-is-a-chakra

What is Reiki, and Does it Really Work? (2021, August 30). Cleveland Clinic. https://health.clevelandclinic.org/reiki/

7 Ways to Strengthen Your Intuition Muscle. (n.d.). Byrdie. https://www.byrdie.com/how-to-strengthen-your-intuition-muscle-5186284

Coughlin, S. (n.d.). We Asked 5 Spiritual Workers To Define "Intuition" — Here's What They Said. Www.refinery29.com. https://www.refinery29.com/en-gb/what-is-intuition-psychic-spiritual-meaning

Highly Intuitive: How Meditation Trains Our Intuition - EOC Institute. (n.d.). Eocinstitute.org. from https://eocinstitute.org/meditation/develop-your-intuition-through-meditation/

Third Eye Chakra Stones: 15 Must-Have Crystals For The Ajna. (n.d.). Tiny Rituals. https://tinyrituals.co/blogs/tiny-rituals/third-eye-chakra-stones

Visualization Meditation: 5 Exercises to Try. (2020, May 28). Healthline. https://www.healthline.com/health/visualization-meditation#:~:text=When%20you%20visualize%2C%20you%20focus

Number 9 Meaning in Numerology. (n.d.). Www.numerology.com. https://www.numerology.com/articles/about-numerology/single-digit-number-9-meaning/

Phillips, D. A. (2015). The complete book of numerology: discovering the inner self. Hay House.

Webster, R. (2002). Pendulum magic for beginners: power to achieve all goals. Llewellyn Publications

Davis-Holmes, K. (2019, March 7). Most Commonly Used Divination Techniques. Woman on Thin Ice. https://kateonthinice.com/10-most-commonly-used-divination-techniques/

WiseWitch. (2018, April 11). Divination: Types and practices. Wise Witches and Witchcraft. https://witchcraftandwitches.com/divination-fortune-telling/divination-types-and-practices/

Dean, L. (2019). The divination handbook: The modern seer's guide to using tarot, crystals, palmistry, and more. Fair Winds Press.

Divination. (2012). In Introduction to Cultural Mathematics (pp. 103–122). John Wiley & Sons, Inc.

Divination: We all just want to know what's coming next. (2018, January 24). Psychology Today. https://www.psychologytoday.com/intl/blog/myth-the-mind/201801/divination-we-all-just-want-know-what-s-coming-next

Nami's guide to crystal divination/crystal throwing. (n.d.). Tumblr https://themanicnami.tumblr.com/post/150142807211/namis-guide-to-crystal-divinationcrystal

Park, G. K., & Gilbert, R. A. (2001). divination. In Encyclopedia Britannica.

Robertson, D. (n.d.). Divination as storytelling: Dealing (with) death and extinction. Open.ac.uk. http://www.open.ac.uk/blogs/religious-studies/?p=1202

Santo, D. E. (2019). Divination. Cambridge Encyclopedia of Anthropology. https://www.anthroencyclopedia.com/entry/divination

The Editors of Encyclopedia Britannica. (2007). crystal gazing. In Encyclopedia Britannica.

Tuczay, C. A. (2015). Magic and Divination. In Set Handbook of Medieval Culture. DE GRUYTER.

Wigington, P. (2010a, January 27). Reading the stones for divination. Learn Religions. https://www.learnreligions.com/divination-with-stones-2561751

Wigington, P. (2010b, September 20). Learn about the basics of numerology. Learn Religions. https://www.learnreligions.com/the-basics-of-numerology-2561761

Wigington, P. (2012, April 4). Methods of Divination. Learn Religions. https://www.learnreligions.com/methods-of-divination-2561764

Wigington, P. (2013, October 12). Bone Divination. Learn Religions. https://www.learnreligions.com/bone-divination-2562499

Wiśniewski, R. (n.d.). Christian divination in late antiquity – Bryn Mawr Classical Review. Brynmawr.edu. https://bmcr.brynmawr.edu/2021/2021.12.13/

Gulino, E. (2020, June 25). There Are 80+ Types Of Astrology. Here's Where To Start. Refinery29.Com; Refinery29. https://www.refinery29.com/en-us/types-of-astrology

Astrology vs Astronomy: What's the Difference? (2014, July 14). Sky & Telescope. https://skyandtelescope.org/astronomy-resources/whats-difference-astrology-vs-astronomy/

Brown, M. (n.d.). What Is Astrology, Actually? InStyle https://www.instyle.com/lifestyle/astrology/what-is-astrology

How You Can Predict Your Future Using Astrology? (n.d.). Streetdirectory.Com. 2022, from https://www.streetdirectory.com/etoday/-uwcalj.html

Garis, M. G. (2020, December 18). The 5 Most Common Mistakes People Make When Reading Their Horoscope, According to an Astrologer. Well+Good. https://www.wellandgood.com/how-read-horoscope/

Understanding the Astrological Chart Wheel. (2018, March 15). Cafeastrology.Com. https://cafeastrology.com/articles/how-to-understand-read-chart-wheel.html

Astrology Symbols and Glyphs. (2015, April 16). Cafeastrology.Com. https://cafeastrology.com/astrology-symbols-glyphs.html

Hall, M. (n.d.). Understand the Basics of Astrology. LiveAbout. https://www.liveabout.com/what-is-astrology-206723

Brown, M. (2022, July 19). Your astrological birth chart, explained. POPSUGAR. https://www.popsugar.com/smart-living/astrology-birth-chart-48875828

DeSimone, M. (2020, August 20). The benefits of getting a birth chart reading. Tarot.com. https://www.tarot.com/astrology/birth-chart-benefits

Hall, M. (2007, March 4). Scorpio moon sign: Personality and characteristics. LiveAbout. https://www.liveabout.com/scorpio-moon-moon-signs-206988

Williams, M. (2022, March 31). What is a birth chart in astrology? Chani Nicholas. https://chaninicholas.com/what-is-a-birth-chart/

Astrogle. (2010, December 17). Origins of Numerology and its usage. Vedic Astrology & Ayurveda. https://www.astrogle.com/numerology/origins-of-numerology-and-its-usage.html

Beltran, M. A. (2020, July 29). Discover the ancient practice of numerology. Thriveglobal.com. https://thriveglobal.com/stories/discover-the-ancient-practice-of-numerology/

Chaldean Numerology. (2021, October 6). GaneshaSpeaks. https://www.ganeshaspeaks.com/numerology/types/chaldean/

Ducie, S. (2017). What is numerology? ReadHowYouWant.com.

Elementually. (2022, April 25). The combined power of astrology and numerology. Witchy Spiritual Stuff. https://witchyspiritualstuff.com/astrology-and-numerology-combined/

History of Numerology. (2021, June 4). MyPandit. https://www.mypandit.com/numerology/history/

History Of Numerology. (2021, October 6). GaneshaSpeaks. https://www.ganeshaspeaks.com/numerology/history/

Hurst, K. (2017, December 18). Numerology: What is Numerology & how does it work? The Law Of Attraction; Cosmic Media LLC. https://thelawofattraction.com/what-is-numerology/

Jain, S. (2022, June 8). Types of numerology number systems and their interpretation. AstroTalk Blog - Online Astrology Consultation with Astrologer; AstroTalk. https://astrotalk.com/astrology-blog/types-of-numerology-number-systems-and-their-interpretation/

Luke. (2020, December 27). How does numerology work with astrology? MIND IS THE MASTER. https://mindisthemaster.com/astrology-and-numerology/

Moon, R. W., & Shadow, C. (2020). Numerology and astrology: 2 Books in 1. The complete collection of books on numerology and astrology for beginners. Includes relationships and dating compatibility, zodiac signs and horoscope. Rdl Publishing.

Printed in Great Britain
by Amazon